D1601426

THE NEW CIVIL WAR

THE NEW CIVIL WAR

Government Competition for Economic Development

Douglas J. Watson

PRAEGER

Westport, Connecticut
London

Library of Congress Cataloging-in-Publication Data

Watson, Douglas J.
The new civil war : government competition for economic development / Douglas J. Watson.
p. cm.
Includes bibliographical references and index.
ISBN 0-275-94788-2 (alk. paper)
1. Urban policy—United States. 2. Community development—United States. 3. Municipal government—United States. 4. Local government—United States. I. Title.
HT123.W36 1995
307.76'0973—dc20 94-22005

British Library Cataloguing in Publication Data is available.

Library of Congress Catalog Card Number: 94-22005
ISBN: 0-275-94788-2

First published in 1995

Praeger Publishers, 88 Post Road West, Westport, CT 06881
An imprint of Greenwood Publishing Group, Inc.

Printed in the United States of America

The paper used in this book complies with the Permanent Paper Standard issued by the National Information Standards Organization (Z39.48-1984).

10 9 8 7 6 5 4 3 2 1

Dedicated to my wife, Patricia E. Watson

Contents

Acknowledgments

I am grateful to a number of people who have given ideas and support to this project. This work grew out of my professional and academic work in the field of economic development and my interest in the political and economic relationships between the public and private sectors.

Several economic development professionals willingly lent their assistance to this project. Phillip Dunlap of Auburn, Alabama, and Jim Byram of Bessemer, Alabama, were especially helpful in providing information and insights in the preparation of the manuscript. David Toenes of Mobile was extremely generous with his time in sharing his knowledge of the U.S. Navy's Gulf Coast homeporting program. Numerous colleagues and friends read various portions of the manuscript and provided insight and criticism that helped to improve it. Of course, I take full responsibility for the final product.

Finally, I am grateful to the members of my family, and particularly my wife, Patricia, for their support and encouragement during my work on this project.

— Douglas J. Watson

THE NEW CIVIL WAR

1 Competitive Governments

During the 1980s, an important shift took place in the relationship between the public and private sectors on the local level in the United States. During the past decade, local officials have become markedly more proactive in their quest to create economic development in their communities than at any other time in this century. They have been innovative in the ways in which they are intervening in the market to assist the private sector in building new businesses and creating jobs in their local areas. Some local governments are now viewed as entrepreneurs in activities that are traditionally considered to be reserved for the private market.

One publication proclaimed:

> The history of cities in the United States is entering a new era of public entrepreneurship. . . . This profound change in the way cities operate may best be termed "urban entrepreneurship." Cities are acting as risk-takers and active competitors in the urban economic game, and the key to each city's success is its ability to invest and to market shrewdly.[1]

There are several explanations for the new, more active role of local governments in economic development activities. The first is the diminished role of the federal government in aiding communities through grants-in-aid. During the Reagan-Bush years, direct federal aid to local governments fell dramatically. Enlightened community leaders realized that the huge federal deficits practically eliminated the possibility of any substantial federal assistance even if the will existed among federal policymakers to provide assistance. The need for local governments to look out for themselves in the strengthening of their own tax bases became apparent. One author aptly identified the new era as "fend-for-yourself federalism."[2]

A second factor was the example provided by the Urban Development Action Grant (UDAG) program, a federal aid program initiated by President Carter in 1977 and terminated finally by President Reagan and the Congress in 1989. The mission of UDAG was to create new jobs in distressed cities and urban counties through public-private partnerships. Local officials were required to negotiate "deals" with private firms to locate or expand in their communities in exchange for low-interest loans, grants, or the construction of needed infrastructure obtained through UDAG. While there were public agencies prior to UDAG playing similar roles in their relationships with the market, UDAG gave proactive economic development a much higher profile by providing the resources to intervene in what are generally considered private sector decisions.

Additionally, UDAGs generally were in the form of low-interest loans to developers, and were to be paid back to the local governments in future years. The Department of Housing and Urban Development (HUD), the federal agency charged with administering the UDAG program, recommended strongly that local governments establish revolving loan funds with the paybacks so that cities and urban counties could continue using the funds to stimulate economic growth in their communities. Of the $2.9 billion loaned to developers during the life of the program, nearly one-third should have been paid back to local governments by 1993.[3]

A third, related factor was the growth in the number of economic development professionals working directly in local government and in agencies sponsored or supported by them.[4] Farr reports that nearly 74 percent of all cities over 10,000 population responding to a survey of the International City-County Management Association either have a department in the local government responsible for economic development or have a public-private partnership formed in the community with the mission of economic development.[5]

Not only was there a growth in the number of professionals working in the field of economic development beginning in the 1980s,[6] there was also a different breed of public employee working in this field. One author describes how the new economic development professional differed from the stereotypical local government employee:

> Urban entrepreneurship entails a new breed of municipal official, transcending the traditional local government roles of delivering

services and enforcing regulations. The city entrepreneurial role includes characteristics traditionally viewed as distinctive to the private sector, such as risk-taking, inventiveness, self-reliance, profit motivation, and promotion.[7]

The conclusion can be drawn that economic development is considered by a large majority of local officials to be a legitimate function of government. As Farr concludes in her study of local economic development: "Involvement in economic development is an integral aspect of local government."[8]

AN APPROPRIATE AND NECESSARY ROLE?

While there does appear to be broad acceptance of the role of local government in economic development activities, the question still arises whether this is both an appropriate and a necessary function for local governments. This issue falls squarely in the debate over the proper role of governments and markets in free-enterprise economies. In Wolf's words, it is "the cardinal policy issue facing modern economic systems."[9]

In the next section, the question of economic development on the local level as an appropriate function of government will be explored. In the following section, the necessity of local economic development will be examined.

Is Local Economic Development Appropriate?

Promarket proponents believe that the market, if left to its own devices, will produce full employment and result in an efficient use of resources on the individual level. Milton Friedman has argued that government should be limited to its "public good" functions, such as defense and law and order, and should not be involved in activities that can be performed by the market.[10] An active government "impairs efficient resource use, impedes economic progress, and restricts social mobility and ultimately political freedom as well."[11] Progovernment advocates, such as J. Kenneth Galbraith in *Age of Uncertainty,* see a need for government intervention in the market to correct market deficiencies. They view "government policy and intervention as essential to bringing about economic stability, efficiency, and enhanced social equity."[12]

One way to address this debate is to place it in the context of theory justifying government intervention in markets in general. One such theory identifies market failures that call for government intervention in situations where the market does not produce certain desirable public goods in sufficient quantity or quality because the costs or benefits are not directly related to the producer of the goods or services. Education, research and development, and national defense are examples of public goods often cited as ones that would not be produced in adequate quantity by the market without government involvement. Second, when monopolies arise, government can intervene in the market to ensure competition.

Third, market failure occurs when there are market imperfections, such as when prices or interest rates do not reflect relative shortages or where information is not equally available to all producers or consumers. And finally, the fourth market failure is distributional equity, which is the market's inability to reduce excessive differences in the distribution of wealth. Redistributive measures, such as income taxes, welfare payments, and unemployment benefits, are used by government to address these equity concerns of society.[13] In each of these cases, government can act to reduce or remove these imperfections in the market.

Is local government intervention in the market through economic development activities justifiable under the "theory of market failure"? This proactive role cannot be founded on the grounds of the failure of the market to produce public goods in adequate supply since local governments address this problem through the provision of numerous services, such as schools and recreation programs. The provision and production of these public goods are generally considered legitimate functions of local government in the United States. In addressing the second and third reasons for government intervention in the market under the theory of market failure, one must conclude that local governments are not involved in breaking up monopolies, nor can they have any effect on prices or interest rates.

However, in the market's failure to distribute its bounty equitably, we find justification for an active role by local governments in economic development. Economic development efforts are aimed at creating new jobs, retaining present jobs, and generating additional taxes in communities that result in stable local economies. If the market does not create jobs or taxes without assistance from local governments, officials justify using public resources to do so. For example, when the housing industry did not build enough low- and moderate-income homes in one community, city leaders created an affordable-housing program with interest-free construction loans to builders, 25 percent second-mortgage loans to qualified applicants, and certain guarantees to banks to induce them to make first-mortgage loans to the buyers. Since the market was not producing new housing for its low- and moderate-income residents, the city felt that intervention in the market was necessary to address the obvious need for decent housing.

Is Local Economic Development Necessary?

Sharp defines economic development as "enhancing growth and sustaining vitality of the local economy, or re-energizing the local economy if it has been subject to decline."[14] This broad definition allows a myriad of different strategies and actions to be undertaken by local governments in the name of economic development. Evidence abounds that numerous actions are justified by local officials because they are done in the name of developing the local job and tax bases. For example, new recreational facilities, such as softball complexes, are constructed because they will fill motel rooms and restaurants. The Retirement Systems of Alabama built an elaborate system of championship golf courses in partnership with several Alabama cities with the justification that they would bring tourists to the state and improve the local economies. They probably would not have had such ready public acceptance if they were sold simply as improved facilities for local golfers.

Does all of this activity on the part of local governments in the name of economic development have a real impact on the growth or stability of local economies? Those opposed to such efforts claim that the market will either produce the new jobs and growth if it is healthy or fail to do so if it is not. Matters such as interest rates and availability of capital are the factors that produce growth, not the efforts of economic development organizations or local governments. Numerous studies have demonstrated that incentives, such as tax-free bonds, have little effect on the location of industries.[15] While the original purpose of industrial development bonds was to attract industry to poorer regions, all states now offer similar incentives, so a competitive edge for any one locality is not likely over an extended period.

David Stockman, the director of the Office of Management and Budget in the Reagan administration, argued against the UDAG program on the basis that the economy does not need stimuli such as that provided by UDAG when it is in an expansionist cycle. He pointed out that UDAG accounted for only 1 percent of the new jobs created in the United States in the early 1980s. Stockman believed that powerful underlying economic and demographic forces are at work in society so that any effort of government to redirect them will meet with little success.[16]

The critics of economic development generally view its effects on a national basis rather than on a local basis. If a factory moves from Ohio to South Carolina, little or no positive effect on the national economy takes place. Jobs are not being created but simply relocated. When the headquarters of the Presbyterian Church (USA) was moved to Louisville, the move did not have an impact on the national economy, because the headquarters already existed in one location and was simply now doing business elsewhere.[17]

The battle in economic development is based not on national policy, but on local competition. Because of the tremendous demographic shifts under way in this country—from Rust Belt to Sun Belt, from inner city to suburbs—there are winners and losers among the nation's localities. Local officials are often judged on their ability to sustain or accelerate economic growth or to reverse misfortune in their economies. Certainly one of the events elected officials relish is the announcement of a major development that will create new jobs and taxes. As a result, there is strong competition among local governments in the area of economic development.

Bowman, in her study of thirty-one southeastern cities, finds the competition ethos of economic development agencies to be "pervasive."[18] She points out that cities cooperate when all can benefit from the outcome; however, when the benefits cannot be shared by all, the incentive to cooperate is removed and cities become competitive with each other. Bowman states, "By virtue of their existence, jurisdictions are self-interested entities. Competition is said to occur when benefits are returned to a subset of the jurisdictions seeking them. Cooperation is precluded by the simple fact that it leads to no joint gains. Self-interest dictates competitive behavior."[19]

Sharp concludes that economic development, by its nature, requires that the key leaders in a community be involved in the nonroutine decisions of committing substantial community resources to a project. Political leaders feel a need to be involved, because the "questions of who gets what and assessments of the winners and losers in economic development tend to focus on city-to-city comparisons."[20] Sharp states that the dominant theme in economic development is competitive and not cooperative, since it "pits communities (and regions) one against the other and forces local officials into an entrepreneurial, risk-taking role that contrasts with the more traditional roles of urban service policymaking and administrative oversight."[21]

The Associated Press reported recently on the competition for economic growth or, in some cases, survival:

> The first War Between the States was fought at Manassas, Gettysburg, Vicksburg, and Shenandoah. The new civil war battlefields have a similar ring: Spartanburg, Indianapolis, Arlington, Ypsilanti, Hoffman Estates.

> This is war—but it's a war fought with incentives, not bullets. A war waged over tax bases, not territory. . . .
>
> "Given the low rate of economic growth and rising unemployment, every mayor and every governor is desperate to get jobs. They are prepared to go some distance to get them," said Clyde Prestowitz of the Economic Strategy Institute.[22]

The competition for economic development has become so intense, and the stakes politically so important, there has been little rational discussion about alternative approaches to growth and recovery. Even though incentives have generally been discredited, there appears to be an escalation in the type and size of incentives offered by state and local governments.[23] For example, ninety cities competed for the $1 billion United Airlines maintenance facility in the early 1990s, with Indianapolis gaining the prize after putting together a nearly $300 million package of incentives.[24]

In their economic development roles, local governments enter the market as sellers competing against other localities for development. The private developer or industry is the buyer and has the luxury of searching the market for the best deals he or she can find. The local government is selling its quality of life, its location, its available sites, its workforce, and various incentives in the same way that a private company sells its products to consumers. Marketing and packaging of the community are as important to economic development as they are to the selling of a product in the marketplace. The buyer, on the other hand, has economic impact to exchange for the community's "products," in the form of permanent jobs, construction jobs, local purchases, new taxes, and the multiplier effect the new business causes throughout the local economy.

There exists substantial evidence in the popular literature that economic development professionals are having success in assisting communities in the growth of their economic bases. Some of these efforts are reported later in the book in the form of case studies. While much of this development would likely have occurred at some point, it may not have taken place in the locations or at the times it did if it had not been for the efforts of entrepreneurial economic developers. For example, an industrial firm may decide that it has sufficient product demand to build a new factory. The fact that it chooses one community over many others vying for the factory may well have to do with the efforts of a local development professional in successfully packaging his or her community.

A second example is the renaissance of several of the nation's large cities' downtown areas during the past decade. The aggressive actions of city governments and their development professionals are credited with the rebirth of dying inner-city business districts. Baltimore's Inner Harbor is an oft-cited case study of how the public and private sectors worked together to revitalize an area cluttered with dilapidated and abandoned warehouses and factories. The Inner Harbor is now one of the leading tourist attractions on the East Coast.[25]

It is difficult to quantify the impact of the efforts of economic developers. However, because economic development is based on competition among localities, it is apparent that some communities are more proficient than others in creating new jobs and taxes. Some cities are realizing substantial returns on the investments they have made in their economic development organizations, while others are not.

Some observers have argued that state and local governments would be better off if they would forget about incentives and invest their money in schools, airports, highways and streets, and cultural and sports facilities. If the quality of life is high in a community, economic growth will take place, the argument goes. This longer-range view, however, is difficult for elected officials to take when they feel they are desperately competing for growth or survival and feel their political futures are dependent on short-term success.

In conclusion, economic development on the local level is probably necessary politically because local officials realize that they are being held accountable for the condition of their local economies by the electorate. In the absence of leadership from the federal or state levels, it is likely that the competition for economic growth will continue to be keen among localities. It is apparent that strategies that appear to work in one place are quickly duplicated in others. Since this is the case, the question of whether the particular strategies employed by local governments are the most effective ones is in need of close examination.

POLITICAL DIMENSIONS OF COMPETITION

It is clear from the popular press and the academic literature that local governments are in competition with each other for economic growth. The highly publicized battles for major new facilities in the United States over the past decade dramatically illustrate the competitive nature of local economic development. The locations of the Saturn plant in Tennessee, the BMW factory in South Carolina, and the United Airlines maintenance terminal in Indiana were seen as major victories for state and local officials in their home areas because they won the competition with other areas for these major economic development prizes. The concessions granted and the incentives offered by the state and local governments to the companies resulted from the competition. The localities were the sellers and the companies were the buyers in the economic development marketplace. Before the companies "bought" the sites they chose, they studied the market very carefully and weighed offers from the various "sellers." For example, the Associated Press reported after United Airlines selected Indiana as its site for the maintenance facility:

> Kentucky folded its hand at $341 million in cash, land and tax abatements. Governor Wallace Wilkinson said United wanted to "prolong it to the point they were sure they had squeezed every drop of blood out of every turnip."
>
> The airline "kept cutting the deal and upping the ante," said Jefferson County Judge-Executive Dave Armstrong.
>
> Indiana Gov. Evan Bayh defended the winning offer as a sound investment that will pay off in long haul, even if the state and Indianapolis have budget shortfalls.[26]

Because of the political significance of economic growth, a relatively large amount of the time of chief elected officials is spent on economic development activities. It is an accepted practice for governors and mayors to travel to other states and nations in search of new industries and other investments. Oftentimes, economic development professionals will enlist the support of chief elected officials to impress upon a company's decision makers how welcome they will be in their jurisdictions. In June 1993, the governor of Alabama flew to Germany to present that state's proposal to Mercedes-Benz, which was considering building a plant in the United States. His trip was not unique but was only one in a long string of visits from American public officials to the executives of the German car maker.

In a content analysis of State of the State addresses by the nation's governors, George Kiser found that economic development was the most popular subject of discussion. Among 200 issues identified in the speeches, jobs and the economy were mentioned 23 percent of the time issues were discussed by the governors. Kiser found that governors often spoke of economic development successes in their speeches and, in particular, were working hard to lure foreign business to their states.[27]

The governor of Kansas may have increased the level of competition when she created the Kansas Cavalry in 1992. The Kansas Cavalry was a group of unpaid Kansas business executives who were enlisted by the governor to target industrial leaders in other states in an effort to have them move their industrial facilities to Kansas. The governor wrote personal letters to chief executive officers of out-of-state firms in which she stated: "I believe that you will be interested in what the Cavalry members have to say about our state and our people. I urge you to set aside a few minutes of your time to meet with them and become better acquainted with the opportunities that Kansas can offer your company."[28] Economic development professionals in states targeted by the Kansas Cavalry expressed their outrage at the action of the Kansas governor to raid their industries.[29]

The competition among the nation's state and local governments for economic development is a good example of laissez-faire economics. There is no regulation on the competition except that elected officials have to sense at what point their offers will no longer be politically acceptable to their constituents. In our federal system, it is unlikely that the federal government will attempt to stop the competition among the states in a meaningful way. It can limit federal tax abatements, such as Congress did in the Tax Reform Act of 1986, and it can require industries to give workers adequate notice before they close their factories and move them to other locations. States would have to agree among themselves to recruit industries through a self-imposed limitation on incentives and other economic development tools. There have been some limited efforts among states to restrict recruiting industries from each other. For example, in 1990, New York, New Jersey, and Connecticut agreed to ban advertisements that attempted to lure businesses from each other.[30] Any widespread agreement appears highly unlikely, however, because of the need for states and localities to pursue their own self-interests.

Will laissez-faire work for the nation's states and localities in economic development, or will it result in excesses that damage local economies and prove counterproductive for the national economy? Babcock has argued that history holds an important lesson for modern entrepreneurial local governments and should be strongly considered so that the current movement does not repeat the failures of the past.[31]

LESSONS FROM THE NINETEENTH CENTURY

In the years prior to the Civil War, one of the purposes of city governments was to invest in private enterprises. Indeed, the formation of many municipal corporations resulted from the need to issue bonds to build canals or railroads in order to encourage development.[32] Joan Williams explains:

> After the Civil War, a typical scenario emerged: an entrepreneur would come into a tiny hamlet with a proposal to construct a railroad. He would tell residents that a railway connection would make their town into a boomtown—so that their farmland would become prime

> urban real estate. To attain the wealth of Midas, all the town had to do was issue bonds to help finance the railroad. Many towns did and the debt of municipalities rose exponentially during the course of the century.[33]

More often than most citizens found acceptable, the promised development did not take place, and the municipality was left with the responsibility of paying off the bonds.

Babcock argues that Pennsylvania was the leading example of public investment in private enterprises. The intense rivalry between Pittsburgh and Philadelphia led to large investments in banks, railroads, bridges, and roads.[34] When graft was discovered in many of these ventures, the Commonwealth passed a constitutional amendment outlawing public investments in private corporations. As a result, Pennsylvania "auctioned off $1,319,730.65 of property, stock, and bonds it held in private enterprise" in 1843.[35]

Pennsylvania was not alone in enacting legislation limiting the roles of municipal corporations in their relationships with the private sector. Babcock notes: "Cities, on the other hand, were expected to deal with matters clearly public—sewer, water, police, and fire protection. Their business was not business, except in a few instances where public health and safety could be involved—such as electricity, trash collecting, and an occasional public swimming pool."[36]

Over the past 50 to 60 years, the strict lines erected between local governments and the private sector have gradually been erased. Even though most states still prohibit the direct investment of public funds into private corporations, they have invented numerous vehicles to accomplish the same task. Most states allow local governments to establish various boards and commissions (for example, industrial development boards) to issue bonds and lend the proceeds to a private industry. Usually these organizations are exempt from numerous other legal requirements that cities face, such as competitive bid laws, open meeting laws, and contract term limits. In effect, they serve as the cities' agents in their dealings with the private sector. Most citizens probably have difficulty recognizing the legal separation of these boards and the city governments that established them. (See chapter 2 for further discussion of this point.)

Babcock warns that the municipality's fiduciary responsibility to citizens conflicts with its role as investor: "It would appear that because the municipality is acting both as investor on the one hand and regulator on the other, an inherent conflict of interest exists that potentially compromises its citizens' best interests."[37]

Should Babcock's warning be heeded? Is the present situation likely to repeat the mistakes from the last century? Should we once again attempt to erect the barriers between what is public and what is private?

One might argue that the situation is much different today than it was in the infancy of the nation. Laws, institutional arrangements, and citizen awareness are much more sophisticated today than they were in the early 1800s. Nevertheless, Babcock's warning should not be ignored, for the competition among localities and states today has the potential to lead to similar abuses.

THE REST OF THE BOOK

The rest of the book attempts to explain why and how this new civil war over economic development is being waged. Chapter 2 relates the ways in which local governments have bypassed the restrictions placed on them to intervene in the private market. It discusses Dillon's Rule and the organizations established outside the traditional structure of local government under laws passed by state legislatures. Some of the more recent weapons of local economic development are discussed. Chapter 3 presents two case studies of small cities that have established successful economic development programs during the past decade. Both cities have employed innovative tools to attract investment and jobs to their communities. The cities' innovation was in response to their determination to be competitive with other cities for the location of companies that built new facilities and created jobs. Chapter 4 examines the state governments' involvement with the competitive efforts of local governments in economic development. Chapter 5 details the decision of the German auto maker Mercedes-Benz to locate a $300 million plant in a small town in Alabama, a case study that illustrates the problems the escalating incentives war causes states. Chapter 6 presents the role the federal government plays in local development, with an emphasis on the competition localities engage in over major federal installations. Chapter 7 is a case study of the U. S. Navy's homeporting program in the 1980s along the Gulf of Mexico. This chapter examines the competition that took place among a number of Gulf Coast cities to attract the Navy's new homeport and the consequences of their efforts. The final chapter is an effort to draw conclusions about competitive governments in the environment of today's "fend-for-yourself" federalism.[38]

NOTES

1. Robert P. Duckworth, John M. Simmons, and Robert H. McNulty, *The Entrepreneurial American City* (Washington, D.C.: Partners for Livable Places and the U.S. Department of Housing and Urban Development, 1986), 4–5.

2. John Shannon, "The Return to Fend-for-Yourself Federalism: The Reagan Mark," *Intergovernmental Perspective* 13 (Summer/Fall 1987): 34–37.

3. David Rymph and Jack Underhill, *Analysis of Income Earned from UDAG Projects* (Washington, D.C.: U.S. Department of Housing and Urban Development, 1990), i.

4. Thomas S. Lyons and Roger E. Hamlin, *Creating an Economic Development Plan* (New York: Praeger Publishers, 1991), 1–2.

5. Cheryl Farr, "Encouraging Local Economic Development: The State of the Practice," in International City Management Association, *The Municipal Year Book 1990* (Washington, D.C.: International City Management Association, 1990), 19.

6. Lyons and Hamlin, 1–2.

7. Duckworth, Simmons, and McNulty, 5.

8. Farr, 15.

9. Charles Wolf, Jr., *Markets or Governments* (Cambridge: MIT Press, 1988), 6.

10. Ibid., 2.

11. Ibid.

12. Ibid., 17–20.

13. Elaine B. Sharp, *Urban Politics and Administration* (New York: Longman, 1990), 216.

14. Thomas J. Moore and Gregory D. Squires, "Industrial Revenue Bonds: The Social Costs and Private Benefits of a Public Subsidy," *Public Administration Quarterly*, 12, no. 2 (Summer 1988), 155.

15. William Greider, *The Education of David Stockman and Other Americans* (New York: E. P. Dutton, 1981), 12.

16. Sharp, 215.

17. Ann O'M. Bowman, "Competition for Economic Development among Southeastern Cities," *Urban Affairs Quarterly*, 23, no. 4 (June 1988), 511.

18. Ibid., 512.

19. Ibid.

20. Sharp, 18.

21. Ibid., 19.

22. Robert Dvorchak, "Business Incentives Incite New Civil War," *Montgomery Advertiser*, 4 October 1992, 1A and 15A.

23. Roger Wilson, *State Business Incentives and Economic Growth: Are They Effective? A Review of the Literature* (Lexington, Ky.: Council of State Governments, 1989): 3.

24. Dvorchak, "Business Incentives Incite New Civil War," 15A.

25. Robert P. Stoker, "Baltimore: The Self-Evaluating City?" in Clarence N. Stone and Heywood T. Sanders, eds., *The Politics of Urban Development* (Lawrence, Kans.: University of Kansas Press, 1987), 244–66.

26. Dvorchak, "Business Incentives Incite New Civil War," 15A.
27. Ellen Shubart, "State by State, 30 Governors Talk Only of Safe Issues," *City & State*, 7 May 1990, 3 and 19.
28. Correspondence from Kansas Governor Joan Finney to President Wyn Thomas of Tru-Flex Metal Hose Corporation, 10 August 1992.
29. Personal discussion with Richard Burger, Economic Development Representative, PSI Energy, Lafayette, Indiana.
30. Dvorchak, "Business Incentives Incite New Civil War," 15A.
31. Richard F. Babcock, "The City as Entrepreneur: Fiscal Wisdom or Regulatory Folly?" in Terry Jill Lassar, ed., *City Deal Making* (Washington, D.C.: Urban Land Institute, 1990), 9–43.
32. Ibid., 9.
33. Ibid., 34.
34. Ibid., 31.
35. Ibid., 11.
36. Ibid., 35.
37. Ibid., 39.
38. Shannon, 34–37.

2 The Weapons of War

In the first chapter, one author was quoted as saying that communities are engaged in a new civil war but that this time the war is fought over economic growth and not with bullets. This war is also not simply a battle between sections of the country, although that element is still present in the struggle to attract or retain manufacturing jobs. This fight is among neighboring communities and communities in other states and other sections of the country. To a large extent, the winners are those that know how to employ the weapons they have at their disposal. Some are provided to them by the federal and state governments, such as tax incentives and training programs; others they create on their own, such as revolving loan funds or incubator programs. Later chapters will discuss some of the programs of the federal and state governments that are available to local governments to assist in economic development. Case studies of the competition among states for a major manufacturing plant and among communities for a federal facility also will be presented. In this chapter, the weapons or tools of economic development created on the local level will be explored.

DILLON'S RULE

A widely accepted doctrine of law in the United States governing the relationship between state and local governments is Dillon's Rule. Enunciated in 1872 by Chief Justice John Forrest Dillon, a justice of the Iowa Supreme Court, Dillon's Rule states simply that local governments can only do what they are expressly authorized to do by the state government. Local governments are not mentioned in the U. S. Constitution, so they are not creatures of the federal government and have no standing legally outside of the powers granted them by the states in which they are located. Since they are created by the states, they are restricted to performing the functions assigned them by state constitutions or legislatures. Except in states where home rule is allowed, local governments are not free to decide to undertake functions outside of those allowed by state law.

Dillon wrote:

> Municipal corporations owe their origin to, and derive their powers and rights wholly from, the legislature. It breathes into them the breath of life, without which they cannot exist. As it creates, so it may destroy. If it may destroy, it may abridge and control.[1]

In chapter 1, some of the abuses by local governments in their relationships with private corporations during the past century were discussed. As we learned, historians believe the misuse of public funds for the benefit of private corporations during that time period resulted in the placement of restrictions on the functions of local governments. Dillon's Rule provided the legal reasoning for the enactment of constitutional amendments and legislative restrictions on the activities of local governments in the late 1800s and early 1900s.[2] For example, the Alabama Constitution of 1901 states:

> The legislature shall not have power to authorize any county, city, town, or other subdivision of this state to lend its credit, or to grant public money or thing of value in aid of, or to any individual, association, or corporation whatsoever, or to become a stockholder in any such corporation, association, or company, by issuing bonds or otherwise.[3]

THE WAY AROUND DILLON'S RULE

Starting in the 1930s, states began to find ways to circumvent the restrictions they had earlier placed on the ability of local governments to intervene in the market by assisting private corporations to invest in their localities. Mississippi, in 1936, authorized the establishment of local industrial development boards (IDBs) and allowed them to issue tax-free bonds to private corporations. Mississippi was anxious to improve its agriculture-based economy with industry it hoped to lure from the North with tax exemptions and cheap labor. The first industrial development bonds were issued in Durant, Mississippi, in 1936 for the Realsilk Hosiery Mills in the amount of $85,000.[4] Kentucky followed Mississippi's lead, in 1946, in granting authority to IDBs to help industry locate in its cities through the issuance of tax-free bonds.[5] When the Mississippi legislation was tested in the U. S. Supreme Court, the Court held that no "substantial federal question was involved."[6] By 1986, all states had passed legislation allowing the formation of local IDBs.[7]

The validity of these statutes was often challenged in state courts. For example, the Kentucky Court of Appeals upheld that state's law in 1950.[8] The typical judicial reasoning for supporting the formation of IDBs and granting them broad powers can be found in the Alabama Supreme Court's decision: "industrial development boards are public corporations which are 'separate entities from the state' and from any political subdivision, including a city or county, within which they are organized."[9]

Industrial development boards have been given broad mandates to assist the private sector in the creation of jobs. Most states have granted IDBs the power to acquire by purchase, lease, gift, exchange, or other means real property and to maintain and furnish it for the use of a private company. Typically, an IDB also can rent property it owns and even "sell, exchange, donate, or convey any or all of its properties whenever its board of directors shall find any such action to be in furtherance of the purposes for which the board was organized."[10] Courts also found it acceptable for local governments to appropriate funds to the IDBs they created to be used for the boards' operations such as the cost involved in recruiting industry and hiring staff.

Probably the most controversial power granted to IDBs is the authority to issue tax-free bonds to help companies build or expand facilities and equip them. Typically, the bonds are sold in the name of the IDB and the proceeds are used to build and equip a facility, such as a manufacturing plant. The IDB retains ownership of the property and leases it to the private company. Once the bonds are retired, ownership of the real property is conveyed to the company for a nominal amount of money. The major advantage of this arrangement is that the company not only receives the lower interest rates associated with tax-free bonds but also is usually exempt from all or some of the property taxes during the time the ownership is in the name of the IDB. Sales and use taxes on the purchase of the materials used in the construction of the facility can also be avoided if the IDB issues purchase orders in its name to buy the materials during construction.[11]

Since the establishment of industrial development boards, states have created numerous other organizations with similar powers in other functional areas. For example, in Alabama, cities have the authority under state law to create downtown development authorities, waterworks boards, medical clinic boards, governmental utility service boards, public building authorities, public library authorities, public athletic authorities, public park and recreation boards, special health care facility authorities, commercial development boards, and others. These boards and authorities have powers to work with the private sector in excess of what the local governments that created them have. As others have noted, this proliferation of responsibility has dealt a harsh blow to governmental accountability to the public and to unified policy making on the local level.[12] However, our purpose in noting the use of boards and authorities is to demonstrate how states, during the past sixty years, have circumvented the earlier restrictions placed on local governments to intervene in the market to create economic development.

Use of industrial revenue bonds, which are also known as industrial development bonds, by the thousands of local boards created in the United States to assist the private sector reached its zenith in the early 1980s. From 1965 to 1985, local tax-exempt bond sales increased from $11.1 billion to $204.3 billion, or a 14.6 percent annual increase over that time period.[13] Competitive governments, anxious for growth in their economies, issued bonds for numerous questionable projects, such as Kmart stores and McDonald's restaurants. In reaction, Congress placed severe restrictions on the use of tax-exempt bonds in the 1986 Tax Reform Act.[14] No longer did cities have broad latitude in the issuance of bonds for commercial development, and they were restricted in the use of bonds even for clearly public purposes.

TRADITIONAL ROLES IN ECONOMIC DEVELOPMENT

The next sections will present some of the latest developments by local governments to gain an advantage in the competition for economic growth. However, before discussing these innovative programs, we note that cities and counties also have expanded their efforts in the more traditional area of providing infrastructure for development. For example, most manufacturing plants now are located in industrial parks developed by local governments. The last generation of industrial facilities in this country was built on separate tracts of land usually close to where workers lived. Localities today are not considered to be competitive in industrial recruitment unless they have a fully developed industrial park. Manufacturing has been zoned out of sections of cities that originally provided for it, so industrial parks are necessary for a city to be able to compete with other communities for new industries.

Other infrastructure is also essential to economic development. Because most businesses are required to meet environmental standards, they look for communities with adequate water, waste water, and solid-waste disposal facilities. In addition, the transportation network serving the community must be adequate to handle the needs of the business. Oftentimes, the industry will require that a new road be constructed to serve a site that will generate significantly more traffic that it did previously.

Local governments have realized how important "quality of life" is in economic development competition. Efforts are made by most cities to improve the appearance of their communities and to offer amenities, such as parks, libraries, and museums. Schools are often important factors in the location of an industry because the company may relocate key executives and their families to the community.

With the extremely competitive situation among jurisdictions to attract businesses, many have developed innovative programs. The next several sections in this chapter will discuss some of the innovative efforts to create economic development by the nation's local governments.

REVOLVING LOAN FUNDS

Federal funds granted to cities and counties for economic development are exempt from the legal restrictions placed on local governments to assist the private sector. The prohibitions cited above apply to locally generated funds and not ones received from the federal government in the form of grants. One federal program, Urban Development Action Grants (UDAG), led to a significant innovation in the way cities and urban counties deal with the private sector. UDAG's broader role in redefining the local economic development function in two innovative cities will be explained in further detail in the next chapter. In this chapter, one of its important by-products—revolving loan funds—will be examined.[15] Revolving loan funds (RLFs) have been defined by one author as "programs with dedicated equity capital that are capable of recycling lendable funds to finance successive generations of projects over an extended period of time."[16]

While RLFs have existed in the public sector at least since Georgia established one in 1937 to help communities build water and sewer facilities,[17] few local governments had the capacity to lend money to private companies for the purpose of creating jobs and encouraging investment. Exceptions, of course, can be found, such as the Philadelphia Industrial Development Corporation, founded in 1958 as a joint venture of the City of Philadelphia and the Greater Philadelphia Chamber of

Commerce. This quasi-public agency created a loan pool, from repaid federal funds and from other sources, that was used to assist private firms through the use of loans and equity investments.[18] It served as a model for the development of the UDAG program by the Carter administration in 1977.

Throughout the life of the UDAG program (1977–1989), officials of HUD, the federal agency that administered the UDAG program, advised cities to establish revolving loan funds for the placement of UDAG funds that would be repaid to them by grantees. UDAG grants were awarded to cities and urban counties by HUD in competition with other communities and, in turn, given or lent to private developers by the cities or urban counties. According to Rymph and Underhill, by the mid-1990s nearly $1 billion will be repaid to cities and urban counties involved in the UDAG program.[19] Another $1.5 billion is due to cities over the life of the UDAG loans. Sixty-three percent of the cities receiving paybacks have established RLFs and nearly half have targeted loans from their RLFs to industrial or commercial projects. The usual standard that cities use to judge whether a project receives assistance from its RLF is job creation. By early 1990, UDAG paybacks invested in RLFs had been used to assist 1,456 recipients to develop 22,479 jobs.[20]

An example of an RLF is the one developed in Plainview, Texas. That city has targeted its RLF to finance the following:

1. Business and industrial acquisitions, construction, conversion, enlargement, repair, modernization, or development costs.
2. Purchase and development of land easements, rights-of-way, buildings, facilities, leases, or materials.
3. Purchase of equipment, machinery, or supplies.
4. Start-up costs, working capital, and reasonable costs including legal fees incurred for services rendered by accountants, and appraisers developing the project and verifying the proper project completion.[21]

Cities with RLFs have an advantage over those without them when both are competing for the same project. For example, one southern city was competing against two other cities located in the Midwest for a plastics molding plant that promised eventually to create 150 new jobs. The company chose the southern city because it was in a position to lend the company $250,000 to complete renovations on a building in the city's industrial park. The loan from the city's RLF was for a twenty-year term at a low rate of interest.

There are numerous potential problems associated with RLFs for cities. Probably the most obvious is the possibility that the fund will not be managed professionally based on clearly defined criteria. If decisions are made to use the funds for political rewards, such as to lend the money for dubious projects based on political connections, the chances are slim that the RLF will have an impact on the local economy. Rymph and Underhill report that "one of every four cities with a closed out or completed UDAG project has received less than is due from either repayments on loans or participation in cash flow."[22] Bankruptcy of the borrowers was a common reason cities did not receive their full paybacks. Cities' quick willingness to renegotiate the terms of the loans was also a factor in the lack of full repayment by private firms to local governments making the loans. RLFs, unlike banking institutions, are not regulated by any outside agency. If loans are made or forgiven for political reasons, the only oversight available is from the media and the public.

SPECULATIVE BUILDINGS

Speculative industrial buildings are ones constructed in the hope of attracting an industrial buyer or a tenant. The first ones were built by private contractors in the 1940s during slow times in the construction business. Since then, local governments have used speculative buildings extensively as a tool to attract industrial prospects to their communities.[23] The early users of speculative buildings were fast-growing metropolitan areas, but now even small rural communities are erecting "spec" buildings with the expectation that an industry will locate there. For example, Green reports that seventeen speculative buildings were constructed in rural Virginia from 1979 to 1990.[24]

Speculative buildings are widely regarded as necessary by local economic developers in their efforts to remain competitive. Green wrote:

> In terms of real estate and most other facets of economic development, there is no substitute for selling something that is real and tangible. Industrial clients are not impressed with what communities are "going to do" but what they have already accomplished. . . . A speculative building tells a client that many of the headaches of building a new facility have been ameliorated and the "critical path" for construction shortened.[25]

Green found that the eleven rural industrial developers in Virginia who were responsible for building speculative buildings were unanimous in their enthusiasm for speculative buildings.[26] Similarly, Foster's national survey of economic developers in communities that had constructed speculative buildings revealed that 97 percent of the respondents believed that the buildings were successful.[27]

The most common type of speculative building constructed is a shell structure without floors, wiring, interior walls, or other finishings. The exterior walls and a roof are built on a graded site, usually in a community's industrial park. If it fits the needs of an industry, it reduces the construction time for an industry by several months. Some local governments have built turnkey buildings that can be occupied immediately. Of course, the greater the level of completion, the less likely the facility will meet the needs of a particular purchaser or tenant. Industries vary significantly in their requirements for floor strength, wiring, office space and configuration, and numerous other details.

Communities finance speculative buildings in different ways. Some are fortunate enough to have private sector investors who are willing to undertake the risk involved in a speculative building. Public utilities oftentimes are involved in speculative building programs and will invest funds in the construction of the buildings. In some cases, the local government will provide the land on which the private sector investor constructs the building. More often than not, the public sector provides the financing for the building in whole or in part. This is especially true in rural areas where private investors are less likely to be found. Green noted that sixteen of the seventeen speculative buildings constructed in rural Virginia were financed in whole (12) or in part (4) by public funds.

Some states have programs that lend funds to match those of local agencies to construct buildings. Generally, the state loans carry very low or no interest until the buildings are sold or leased. Foster reported that state laws generally limit the states' participation to no greater than 50 percent of the total cost of the building.[28] Alabama law, for example, limits the state share to no greater than 25 percent of the total cost of the building.[29]

A fairly high number of speculative buildings are not sold but are leased to industries, even though most communities prefer to sell their buildings so that they may recover their cash investment and use it for other purposes. In a study of six Alabama cities that constructed eighteen speculative buildings, the authors found that none of the buildings had been sold. Six were under construction at the time of the study, two were unoccupied, and ten were leased.[30]

Some cities have developed policies that allow them to build industrial buildings to suit prospective industries. The buildings are then leased to the industry generally with the option to purchase. If a city has capitalized its building fund, it has the ability to make very attractive terms available in order to outbid other localities that are competing for the same development. An example of an active build-to-suit program is that of Bessemer, Alabama, described in detail in chapter 3.

Apparently, little empirical exploration of the utility of speculative buildings as a useful economic development tool has been made. Oftentimes, the commitment of the funds for speculative buildings is based on the advice of state officials who encourage local governments to have available buildings to show to industrial prospects. At other times, officials notice other communities have had success in attracting industries with speculative buildings, so they believe that their community must also have one in order to be competitive. Studies in the economic development literature generally have been limited to reports of the favorable opinions of economic developers who have been involved in the construction of speculative facilities. It is beyond the scope of this book to determine whether speculative buildings are worthwhile or not; however, it is interesting to note that local governments are willing to invest hundreds of thousands of dollars because they believe that speculative buildings make them competitive with other communities.

The result of speculative building and build-to-suit programs is that local governments or their representatives are now in the real estate business as lessors of industrial buildings. Local governments are playing a role traditionally reserved for the private real estate market. This role is quite different from the limited one envisioned for local governments by the proponents of Dillon's Rule. Local governments have moved considerably beyond simply providing infrastructure and regulating the development process. The leaders of competitive governments apparently believe that such actions are necessary if they are to get a share of industrial locations.

SPECIAL ATTRACTIONS

City leaders have invested heavily in facilities that they believe make their communities attractive to tourists and to their own citizens who have money to spend on leisure activities. The construction of these special attractions has often been linked to other community goals, such as the revitalization of downtowns. In many cases, these projects involve complicated partnerships between public and private entities. It is not unusual for there to be several public agencies, including not-for-profit development groups, involved with private developers. In some cases, authority from state legislatures is required before a project can go forward.

As with many other local economic development efforts, apparent success in one city leads to numerous similar projects in other cities. In the following paragraphs, several examples are given of cities taking the lead in providing special attractions with the expectation that they will lead to economic vitality. In each case, other cities have taken steps to replicate the innovative city's project.

In the late 1980s and early 1990s, a number of large American cities competed for the right to have expansion teams from either the National Football League or Major League Baseball. Referenda were approved for the construction of major facilities, such as new stadiums in Baltimore and Denver. St. Petersburg even went so far as to build a new speculative domed stadium for $234 million to make that city more attractive for professional sports. Atlanta competed for the 1996 Olympics and pledged to build new facilities to handle the numerous events. When the Olympics are over, Atlanta will use the new stadium for its professional baseball team.[31] In the early 1990s, Atlanta built the Georgia Dome that serves as home for its professional football team.

Cooper points out that, in addition to professional sports facilities, other attractions—such as convention centers, aquariums, and waterfront projects—have all been popular with large cities in their efforts to stimulate their economic bases.[32] While some have been successful, others have not fared well in realizing a return on taxpayers' investments. Interesting examples are the downtown festival marketplaces constructed in a number of American cities during the 1970s and 1980s.

Boston's Faneuil Hall Marketplace was built by the Rouse Corporation and the city of Boston in 1976. Its success in transforming the dilapidated buildings on Boston's waterfront into a major commercial and tourist center inspired other cities to follow suit. Baltimore's Inner Harbor was another widely acclaimed success story for the city of Baltimore and Rouse. However, other projects, such as the ones in Richmond and Toledo, were failures in the sense that they will probably never make a profit.[33] In her analysis of six major festival marketplaces, Achs points out that local governments invested heavily in these projects and only Boston has shown a financial return on investment.[34] However, the value of these projects cannot be measured strictly in return on investment. The successes of the Faneuil Hall Marketplace and the Inner Harbor have created a sense of community pride in each city and have led to other investments in the downtowns of Boston and Baltimore.

Smaller cities have also invested heavily in special attractions that they believe will result in economic growth. With the immense popularity of softball, many small cities have spent millions developing softball complexes that can host tournaments on summer weekends. Thousands of players and their families are attracted to the tournaments and stay in local motels and eat in restaurants. Generally, local officials and taxpayers support the construction of these facilities because of the potential for economic development rather than the improvement they make to local recreation programs.

Other examples of using sports facilities as the bases for economic growth in smaller or medium-sized cities are water parks and golf courses. Dothan, Alabama, has successfully developed a combination water theme park and softball complex utilizing tax revenue on motels and hotels to pay the debt service on the facility. South Carolina's Grand Strand area has numerous golf courses that are used to lure visitors in the summer months from colder climates. The Robert Trent Jones Golf Trail in Alabama is a similar effort to bring golfers to the state to play the courses built jointly by five cities and the Retirement Systems of Alabama.

It is likely that cities will continue to invest in special-attraction facilities in the expectation that they will generate economic growth. Sometimes cities invest in these facilities rather than in more traditional infrastructure. In one small southern city, after millions of dollars were invested in the construction of a major new golf facility, citizens complained that there had been no street resurfacing for several years except for the roads leading to the new facility. However, as Cooper concludes, "[M]ayors wisely recognize what a lot of community activists don't: The public usually likes these big showy projects and won't forego them in order to sink more money into, say, wasteful school systems."[35]

BUSINESS INCUBATORS AND RESEARCH PARKS

In the early days of competition for industrial development, almost all efforts of state and local governments were directed toward attracting industries that were relocating from other sections of the country or were building satellite facilities in addition to their existing plants. The provision of industrial revenue bonds in the 1930s and 1940s by southern states to companies willing to build plants there illustrates the emphasis on the recruitment of outside industry. For the most part, there was little heavy industry in the South, and state and local leaders believed that manufacturing jobs had to be added to their economies if they were to eliminate the high level of abject poverty existing among their citizens. In 1936, the Mississippi legislature enacted that state's Balance Agriculture with Industry (BAWI) program, which contained the first state subsidies to industries to attract them to relocate from one state to another.[36] To a large degree, this strategy of attracting industrial growth to the South has been successful over the past fifty years.

While all states and most local governments now compete for new manufacturing facilities (as has been described previously), many have realized that the potential for significant economic growth may exist in their own communities. Each year, thousands of small businesses are started in this country and a high percentage of them fail. Oftentimes they fail because they are undercapitalized and they simply cannot afford the overhead costs involved in starting a new business, especially one that manufactures a product. Manufacturing generally requires expensive machinery, a trained workforce, and an adequate building.

In the 1980s, a number of communities decided that they would try to help manufacturers or other types of businesses during the very difficult start-up period. One of the means of providing that help was through the development of incubator programs. In such programs, some governmental agency, university, or community group provides a building or buildings in which several start-up businesses may be co-located at below-market rental rates. Oftentimes, there is shared secretarial help available for the tenants to be used when they need it. Telephones, photocopiers, fax machines, and other office needs are often provided to the fledgling companies. The tenants in an incubator program usually have a "graduation" requirement—that is, they must become viable businesses so that they can exist outside the incubator within several years. The community that provides the opportunity for the business to grow in its incubator generally expects the company to build its business facility there after graduation and provide jobs for its citizens. Many of the successful incubator programs have been developed in association with major universities and are often part of a research park geared to fostering the development of new technologies. For example, in 1986 the city of Evanston, Illinois, and Northwestern University opened an incubator in an 11,000 square foot building, added 6,000 square feet more in 1988, and 35,000 square feet more in 1990. The university owns the incubator and manages it as a department of the university.[37] The thirty start-up businesses that occupy the incubator space are provided business and technical assistance from the Technology Commercialization Center that is housed in the incubator. The Technology Commercialization Center acts "as a broker of university services to technology based businesses . . . and [provides] assistance to university faculty [members who] wished to commercialize their technology."[38]

A second example of a university-based incubator program as part of a research park is the one that was created by the city of New Haven, a large private sector firm (Olin Industries), and Yale University. The New Haven Science Park was developed on an abandoned eighty-acre site donated by Olin Industries and consists of five buildings totaling 400,000 square feet. Among the five buildings are incubators owned by the Science Park that employ approximately 500 people. According to Palmintera, the New Haven incubator program has focused on technology-based start-ups. Eighty percent of the firms in the incubator program are technical businesses and 20 percent are support services for the technical tenants.[39]

Palmintera's description of the services of the Science Park illustrates the benefits provided to the tenants of a well-run incubator program:

> The park provides a range of assistance to tenants, including shared administrative services and group insurance plans. There is an in-house consulting operation called Science Park Associates that provides some free management consulting to incubator firms. Other services, provided free or for a small fee, include business and market planning, referral to service providers, assistance in obtaining public grants or tax incentives such as enterprise zone benefits; assistance in establishing joint ventures; introduction to local venture capitalists; proposal packaging . . . ; and help in interfacing with other sources of funding and assistance. In addition to the services provided by the Science Park Associates, the state recently established a "Business Outreach" program at the park. This business center is designed to assist small firms with business and marketing plans and small business packaging. The science park also sponsors monthly luncheons and seminars on business planning and management, financing, technology transfer and other topics of interest to the tenants. Cocktail parties and other social events are held to allow tenants to interact with Yale University professors and others. A bi-weekly newsletter provides other information on financing, management, and technical resources.[40]

The involvement of universities in incubator programs is especially important where the transfer of new technology to commercial applications is a goal. Major research universities, such as Northwestern and Yale, are developing many of the products that will provide employment in the future. Incubator programs are oftentimes the vehicles for start-up companies to commercialize exciting new technologies developed in the laboratories of the nation's major research universities. For example, the city of Auburn, Alabama, and Auburn University operate a technology-based incubator with eight tenants in its 32,000 square feet. Six of the eight companies in the incubator are there because of research produced at Auburn. A more detailed description of the Auburn incubator is presented in chapter 3.

Another example of university involvement with a local government in industrial development is that of North Greenbush, New York, and

Rensselaer Polytechnic Institute. The *Wall Street Journal* reported on this interesting partnership:

> Then in 1983, Rensselaer Polytechnic Institute opened a 1,200-acre high-technology park in town. But young would-be entrepreneurs, many nurtured in Rensselaer's "incubator" program for high-tech businesses, said they couldn't find start-up money. . . . The town set up the venture fund using a $750,000 Department of Housing and Urban Development economic development grant. That money is invested in eight start-up companies, including a biotechnology concern and a computer networking system.[41]

Unlike most private venture funds, the town did not demand a seat on the boards of directors, nor did it require the companies to give it equity positions in the event they succeeded. The town's primary interest was in locating the businesses in the Rensselaer high-tech park. However, officials expect the investments to result eventually in 1,500 new jobs and even more economic growth in support businesses.

Purdue University developed a research park in 1961 that serves as the industrial park for the city of West Lafayette, Indiana. Unlike the programs at Yale, Rensselaer, and Auburn, the city is not involved directly in the ownership or operation of the park but does provide tax exemptions for industries that the university locates. The park consists of over 650 acres of university-owned land housing more than fifty-five companies that employ in excess of 2,000 people.[42] The research park was created by the university so that industry and business could interact with the university "through applied research via the joint efforts of University and industry staff, access to technological and educational resources, and availability of research and development 'incubator' facilities."[43]

Within the Purdue Research Park is the Business and Technology Center that functions as an incubator for small companies. The Purdue incubator has been successful in developing a number of the companies located in the park. For example, in 1981, university researchers developed a heart pacemaker that adjusts pulse rates in response to increased activity by the person using it. The pacemaker development led to the opening of MED Institute, a company specializing in medical technology research located in the park.

Purdue, in more recent years, has tried to limit the industries in the park to companies that have an association with the university. The Purdue Research Foundation, the arm of the university that owns and manages the park, has developed specific guidelines to use when considering whether to allow a company to locate in its park:

- The business or industry will have a technical aspect to its character that will suggest an important relationship with one or more University academic units.
- Limited manufacturing activities are permitted, but there should be a strong technical component to the company's activity.
- Research interaction between the company and the University should be a fundamental part of the company's strategy.
- Internships, co-op student programs, and on-site faculty and graduate student research should be encouraged by the company. In addition, the company should be willing to permit academically qualified staff to serve as adjunct faculty at the University.
- The company should plan to utilize University facilities in [its] technical activities.
- The physical facilities that the company plans to construct in the Park should be commensurate with those of a technically advanced organization.
- Purdue Research Foundation views companies in the Park as partners in a project to develop a technologically advanced community. Therefore, each project will be considered to be part of a long-term commitment on the part of the company and the Foundation.[44]

Purdue University views the park as an asset in several ways. Leroy Silva, director of the Business and Industrial Center at Purdue, cited four reasons why the research park is important to Purdue: (1) it provides opportunities for the faculty to earn extra income through consulting, (2) employment opportunities are created for spouses of faculty and graduate students, (3) students have part-time jobs available with many of the companies in the park, and (4) the location of a high-technology industry next to the university has a positive "environmental influence" because it enhances the university's image as a center for technology research.[45]

Silva stated that the reasons companies desired to locate in the university's park were that the "technological depth or reservoir at a major research university was not found elsewhere" and that the cultural aspects of universities were attractive to executives.[46] The advantage to the city of West Lafayette is that it has not had to make a major investment in the construction of industrial park facilities or in staff salaries for its economic development activities. If there is a disadvantage for the community, it is that the city has no control over the type or amount of industrial development taking place within its borders.

With the increasing emphasis on competition among nations, states, and communities for economic growth, it is likely that research parks and incubators will become even more popular. The United States is generally conceded to have the finest university research facilities and programs in the world; however, there has been a recognition that it has not successfully commercialized in a timely manner the technology developed at its major research universities.[47] Business incubators and research parks associated with major universities promise "to accelerate the transfer of technology from university laboratories to the production line."[48] As industries locate around universities that are offering assistance in the commercialization of research, other universities will feel pressured to compete in order to attract the financial support from industries needing research, as well as to be attractive places to work for the most capable faculty. The most likely form of that competition will be research parks and business incubators, many of them constructed in association with local governments hungry for economic development success.

Luger and Goldstein, in the most exhaustive research done to date on research parks, caution cities and universities against investing too heavily in the development of new research parks.[49] Several of the best-known research parks, such as the Stanford Research Park and the Research Triangle Park, have inspired numerous imitators across the country. According to Luger and Goldstein, there were 116 research parks in 1991, most of which were associated with a university. The development of parks has taken place in "regions whose economies were disproportionately concentrated in slow-growth or declining industries."[50] The authors also found that research parks have "proliferated as a result of competition among branches of state universities. . . . Legislative politics often makes it easier to spread state government investments in research parks among several campuses."[51]

Luger and Goldstein's research indicates that the presence of a major research institution, such as a university or federal research facility, is critical to the success of research parks. The same authors, in a separate journal article, explored the viability of research parks in nonmetropolitan areas and concluded: "Although larger metropolitan areas provide more suitable conditions for research parks to be successful in stimulating the regional economy, the performance to date indicates that research parks in smaller areas with established research universities and/or federal government laboratories can be successful as well."[52] Goldstein and Luger suggest that regions that are unlikely to attract sufficient numbers of scientists and engineers to support a research park should explore other types of economic development. These other efforts, such as manufacturing modernization or labor retraining, could prove to be more cost effective and distribute benefits more evenly among various income groups.[53]

Research parks, then, are not the economic development answer for every community. Leaders of communities that do not have the assets identified by Luger and Goldstein for development of successful research parks should not fall into the "high-tech trap." Because research parks are costly and generally are slow to develop, it would be wiser for most communities to build more traditional industrial parks or to use their resources to strengthen existing sectors of their local economies.

CONCLUSION

There are numerous variations on the efforts that local governments are making to be competitive with other communities. Some of the programs are innovative ones that develop from recognition of unique local opportunities, a good example being the venture fund created by North Greenbush when Rensselaer Polytechnic Institute located its high-tech park there. Other examples are the duplications by some cities of the apparent successes of other cities, such as happened with festival marketplaces. At any rate, local governments are committing sizable portions of their resources to projects and programs that they believe will result in economic growth. These efforts indicate that local leaders have assumed that they have responsibility for the economic futures of their communities.

NOTES

1. Anwar Syed, *The Political Theory of American Local Government* (New York: Random House, 1969), 68.
2. Richard F. Babcock, "The City as Entrepreneur: Fiscal Wisdom or Regulatory Folly?" in Terry Jill Lassar, ed., *City Deal Making* (Washington, D.C.: Urban Land Institute, 1990), 9–43.
3. Alabama Constitution of 1901, Article IV, Section 94, Volume I, 247.
4. Mark Rollinson, *Small Issue Industrial Development Bonds* (Chicago: Capital Publishing Co., 1976), 16.
5. Ibid.
6. Ibid.
7. Douglas J. Watson and Thomas Vocino, "The Changing Nature of Intergovernmental Fiscal Relationships: The Impact of the 1986 Tax Reform Act on State and Local Governments," *Public Administration Review* 50, no. 4 (July–August 1990), 428.

8. Rollinson, 16, 53.

9. *George A. Fuller Company v. Vulcan Materials Company*, 293 Ala. 199, 301 So.2nd 74 (1974).

10. Code of Alabama (1975), Section 11-54-87.

11. Watson and Vocino, 428.

12. See Robert G. Smith, *Public Authorities in Urban Areas: A Case Study of Special-District Government* (Washington, D.C.: National Association of Counties, 1969); Advisory Commission on Intergovernmental Relations, *Regional Decision Making: New Strategies for Sub-state Districts* (Washington, D.C.: U. S. Government Printing Office, 1973); John J. Harrigan, *Political Change in the Metropolis*, 3d ed. (Boston: Little, Brown, 1985), 265, 271.

13. Lillian Rymarowicz and Dennis Zimmerman, "Federal Budget and Tax Policy and the State-Local Sector: Retrenchment in the 1980s," *CRS Report for Congress* (Washington, D.C.: Library of Congress, 9 September 1988), 2. See also Watson and Vocino, 428.

14. For a discussion of the Tax Reform Act, see Watson and Vocino, 427–34.

15. For examples of how cities established revolving loan funds, see International City Management Association, *Recycling CDBG and UDAG Funds* (Washington, D.C.: Management Information Publications, 1991), for examples of how cities established revolving loan funds.

16. John Peterson, Susan Robinson, Percy Aguila, Joni Leithe, and William Graham, *Credit Pooling to Finance Infrastructure: An Examination of State Bond Banks, Revolving Loan Funds, and Substate Credit Pools* (Washington, DC: Government Finance Research Center, 1988), 61.

17. T. Phillip Dunlap, Bettye B. Burkhalter, Douglas J. Watson, and Jacki A. Fitzpatrick, "Reshaping the Local Economy through a Revolving Loan Fund (RLF) in an Entrepreneurial City," *Economic Development Quarterly* (forthcoming).

18. Douglas J. Watson, John G. Heilman, and Robert S. Montjoy, *The Politics of Redistributing Urban Aid* (Westport, Conn.: Praeger Publishers, 1994), ch. 3.

19. David Rymph and Jack Underhill, *An Analysis of the Income Cities Earn from UDAG Projects* (Washington, D.C.: Department of Housing and Urban Development, 1990), i.

20. Ibid., i–ii.

21. International City Management Association, 27.

22. Rymph and Underhill, i.

23. H. McKinley Conway, *Marketing Industrial Buildings and Sites* (Atlanta: Conway Publications, 1980), 264.

24. C. Warren Green, Jr., "Shell Building Experiences of Eleven Rural Virginia Communities: 1979–1990," *Economic Development Review* 9, no. 4 (Fall 1991), 78.

25. Ibid.

26. Ibid., 79.

27. Wayne Foster, *Speculative Buildings: A Tool for Industrial Development* (Jackson, Miss.: Mississippi Research and Development Center, 1977), 3.

28. Ibid., 12–13.

29. Act No. 83-925, Alabama Legislature, 212.

30. Bettye B. Burkhalter, Douglas J. Watson, and Jamie Sinclair, "The Role of Speculative Buildings in Small Community Industrial Recruitment" (Auburn, Ala.: Economic Development Institute, 1991), 24.

31. John Head, "At Last, A Stadium Worthy of Baseball," *Atlanta Journal and Atlanta Constitution*, 26 April 1992, G1 and G3.

32. Matthew Cooper, "Squeeze Play," *Washington Monthly,* June 1993, 50.

33. Nicole Achs, "Putting the Fun(ds) Back into Downtown," *American City and County* (June 1991), 75.

34. Ibid.

35. Cooper, "Squeeze Play," 50.

36. James C. Cobb, *The Selling of the South* (Urbana, IL: University of Illinois Press, 1993), 5–34.

37. Diane Palmintera, *Local- and Regional-based Initiatives to Increase Productivity, Technology, and Innovation* (Washington, D.C.: Innovation Associates, 1991), 105.

38. Ibid., 102.

39. Ibid., 109.

40. Ibid.

41. Lynn Asinof, "Small Town Decides Best Way to Lure High-Tech Firms Is to Invest in Them," *Wall Street Journal*, 6 November 1992, A5.

42. Wendy Togneri, "Research Park Brings New Economic Forces to Purdue, Lafayette," *Lafayette Leader*, 22 October 1993, 3b.

43. Purdue Research Foundation, "Connecting Research and Resources," brochure on Purdue Research Park.

44. Ibid.

45. Interview with Dr. Leroy Silva, director of Business and Industrial Development Center, Purdue University, 13 December 1993, West Lafayette, Indiana.

46. Ibid.

47. William Ihlanfeldt, "Accelerating the Commercialization of Technology through the Research Park Initiative," publication of Research Park, Inc., Evanston, Illinois.

48. Ibid.

49. Michael I. Luger and Harvey A. Goldstein, *Technology in the Garden* (Chapel Hill, N.C.: University of North Carolina Press, 1991), 181–83.

50. Ibid., xvi.

51. Ibid.

52. Harvey A. Goldstein and Michael I. Luger, "University-based Research Parks as a Rural Development Strategy," *Policy Studies Journal* 20, no. 2 (1992), 260.

53. Ibid., 261.

3 Joining Battle: Two Competitive Cities

In the first two chapters, reasons were advanced for the changing roles of local governments in economic development over the past twenty years. Chapter 1 discussed the lessening of federal funds to address local problems, the existence of the Urban Development Action Grant program, and the changing national economy as factors that have influenced how local governments view their roles in developing jobs. Chapter 2 pointed to an additional reason for this changed role for local governments: the competition among them to attract investment that creates jobs. Here we consider this argument more directly.

The competition for the limited number of new jobs created in this country each year, especially in manufacturing, has been an important factor in the increased emphasis on economic development among local governments. Whether this more active role in economic development is a legitimate one has been strongly debated in the public administration and the public policy literature.[1] Regardless of philosophical objections to it, local governments are deeply involved in economic development and are likely to remain so for the remainder of the twentieth century.

In order to present a clearer picture of the types of efforts used by local governments to be competitive in the attraction of investment and the creation of jobs, we have chosen to present case studies of two small cities that are recognized as having successful, comprehensive economic development programs. Both cities have worked aggressively with the private sector to offer incentives and provide infrastructure that have made them attractive places to invest. One of the cities is an academic community that did not have any manufacturing plants twenty years ago.

Community leaders decided that the economic base of the city should be expanded to include industries that were compatible with the major university located in the city. This case study discusses that community's efforts to attract environment-friendly industries as well as to promote an expanded commercial sector.

The second city developed as a home for heavy industry, specifically, steel plants. When the American steel business suffered from foreign competition in the 1970s, this industrial city faced a serious decline in employment and other economic factors. This case study tells the dramatic story of how the community established an organization in the 1980s to bring new industrial and commercial enterprises to the city.

AUBURN: AN ACADEMIC COMMUNITY DIVERSIFIES

Until the mid-1970s, Auburn, Alabama, was content to be an academic community as home to the state's largest university. Auburn University, a land grant university in Alabama, provided a solid economic base for the community that made it mostly immune to the fluctuations of the state and national economies. Its 8,000 employees, 21,000 students, and $350 million budget provided local businesses in the city of 34,000 residents with stable customers in somewhat of a captive market. The nearest larger cities are Montgomery, 60 miles to the west; Columbus, Georgia, 30 miles to the east; and Birmingham and Atlanta, both approximately 100 miles to the north, so Auburn residents or students who desired to trade elsewhere had to commute a fair distance to do so. The bookstores, restaurants, and other businesses that catered to students and faculty members prospered.

Phase 1: Getting Started

In the mid-1970s, a group of businessmen decided that the community should diversify its economy in order to lessen its dependence on the university. They proposed that an industrial development board (IDB) be established by the city council, with its membership composed of prominent businessmen in the community. Furthermore, the city council was asked to contract with the local Chamber of Commerce to provide staff support for the IDB. The city council complied with this request and turned over the industrial development function to the IDB.

Within a short period of time, the IDB asked the city council to purchase a 100+ acre site on the western tip of the city and install the necessary infrastructure for the city's first industrial park. After the park was built in the mid-1970s, the IDB began work necessary for attracting a manufacturing facility to the community. The IDB chairman and the Chamber executive director contacted the Alabama Development Office, the state's industry-seeking agency, and the Alabama Power Company, the state's largest utility, which is very active in industrial development. Representatives of both agencies were shown the industrial park by IDB members. They advised the IDB on how to handle prospects when they were brought to the community.

Before actively considering any potential industries, the IDB members agreed informally on certain criteria an industry must meet in order to locate in Auburn. First, the industry could not have a smokestack or have effluent that polluted the water in any significant way. Board members were cognizant of the nature of the academic community and did not feel industries that caused air or water pollution would be accepted by the citizens of the community who, for the most part, enjoyed stable jobs with the university. Second, the IDB members agreed that they were not interested in companies that would bring unions with them. The city did not have organized labor among any of its existing employers at the time. Over the years, the chairman of the IDB informed prospects of this interest of the IDB early in the recruiting process. Since many of the industries were seeking a new start in the South away from union problems at their northern plants, this condition was generally met with positive reaction by the industrial site locators.

Third, the IDB informed the state and the power company that it was not interested in recruiting industries that would employ more than 500 people. The city's industrial development goal was to attract a number of smaller industries so that the community would not be dependent on any one industry in case of failure. Since the city had the economic stability of a major public institution, it was not in any need of a quick economic fix, and so it patiently adhered to the criteria that the IDB established.

By 1980, the IDB had met with some success with the locations of several industries in the industrial park. This success led the city to double the size of the park. All of Auburn's early industries had several things in common: Most were relocations from northern states, primarily Illinois, Michigan, and Wisconsin; none were larger than 500 employees; none had any serious pollution emissions, either in the air or in the waste water; and all were union free. Apparently there was strong community support for the work of the IDB even though most of the newly employed people in the industries lived in the five-county region surrounding Auburn and not in the city.

During the 1970s, the community's commercial base also began to expand with the construction of the first indoor shopping mall and several more shopping centers that made Auburn the region's retail center. Auburn University experienced unprecedented expansion during this time, which provided more students and faculty as customers for the retailers, bankers, and other businesses in Auburn.

However, by the early 1980s, the national economy had suffered for several years with extremely high interest rates that slowed down the industrial and commercial expansion in Auburn. The primary economic activity under way in the community at that time was the construction of new student apartments that investors were able to use as tax shelters.

During this first phase of economic expansion, the city government played a minimal role. The city council established the IDB, built the industrial parks, and granted tax abatements to industries brought to it by the IDB. The members of the IDB operated outside the city government whenever it could and believed the city council and the city's management had little role in industrial development. Likewise, the city government did not actively work with commercial developers who constructed the new shopping centers in the community. Rather, the government's role was one of reaction to developers once they brought site plans to the city to be approved for zoning. Control for development was clearly in the hands of the private sector. The businessmen who were members of the IDB and the Chamber of Commerce determined the city's industrial development policy and strategy with little or no direction from elected officials.

Phase 2: Establishing Credibility

A new phase of economic development in Auburn began in 1984 when the city council and the city manager decided that they wanted a more active role. The time was right for an increased role for city leaders. There had not been a new industry to locate in the industrial park for several years, and criticism began to appear that not enough was being done in industrial development. Also, the long-time executive director of the Chamber of Commerce who had played a key role in industrial development decided to retire. The city council committed to hiring an economic developer who would work with the Chamber and the IDB in industrial development. However, arrangements with the Chamber did not work out as originally planned, so the city council agreed to hire its own economic developer who would serve as staff to the IDB. This decision had the effect of moving the industrial development function from the Chamber into the city government.

Following a lengthy recruitment process, the city manager hired Phillip Dunlap, who had developed a reputation as one of the nation's leading experts in the UDAG program while working for the city of Birmingham, Alabama. Dunlap had worked for Birmingham for ten years, mostly as a federal grantsman. From 1977 to 1984, he was assigned to develop projects with the private sector to submit to HUD for funding under the UDAG program. His background in banking gave him the tools to create innovative public-private partnerships that resulted in millions of dollars pouring into Birmingham through UDAG. Since Auburn had just been accepted by HUD for eligibility in the UDAG program, Dunlap's experience in working with the private sector to develop successful UDAG applications was especially appealing to the city manager.

Dunlap's initial task was to nurture a working relationship with the business community. The election of a new mayor in 1980 and the selection of a new city manager in 1982 had improved the image of the city in the business community. However, the city had never taken a leadership role in economic development policy or programs. Dunlap's familiarity with the programs of the state and federal governments became an immediate asset for businesspeople who were seeking help in expanding their facilities or workforces. His expertise in the UDAG program proved to be extremely beneficial to the city. Over the five years of the city's eligibility for UDAG (1984–1989), Dunlap brought well over $10 million into the community through that program and the related Housing Development Action Grant program.

The first UDAG was to provide second mortgages to low- and moderate-income citizens so that they could purchase 114 new homes constructed in Auburn under this program. This initial housing program worked in this way: The private builder constructed the home, found an eligible purchaser who qualified for a first-mortgage loan from a local bank, and submitted the application to the economic development director. If the buyer met all the requirements of the program, then he or she would be given a second mortgage equivalent to 25 percent of the cost of the home. If the buyer sold the house before the first mortgage was paid off, then the second mortgage was due at that time. By 1993, the city had already recovered over $400,000 of the $1.4 million UDAG funds used as second mortgages.

A second UDAG project was the construction of a five-story, 90,000 square foot, mixed-use building in the downtown. Two local developers had owned a large vacant lot in the downtown for years but had never been able to construct the office/retail/apartment building on it that they had wanted. With the help of the UDAG packaged by Dunlap, the developers invested nearly $4 million and created sixty-one new jobs in the downtown. The new building also produced an estimated $33,000 in new taxes for the city. In conjunction with this project, the city constructed a parking deck and leased many of the spaces to a bank that occupied one-half of the commercial space and to other tenants in the building. Several years after the building opened, a large utility leased nearly one floor of the building and moved its engineering department there from another city.

A third UDAG project was the construction of a 250-room hotel and 30,000 square foot conference center across from the university campus. Dunlap secured an $858,170 UDAG and arranged for tax-free financing for the project through the IDB. The university leased and managed the conference center, while the developer of the hotel hired a management firm to run the hotel. The terms of the UDAG were very favorable for the city, since the full amount of the UDAG had to be paid back to the city within five years. In addition, more than 175 new jobs were created, mostly for low- and moderate-income residents, and in excess of $150,000 in new taxes were generated by this one project. The hotel fulfilled the community's long-time need for a quality facility and brought thousands of visitors to the city for university-sponsored conferences. Prior to the construction of this facility, the university held its conferences in other cities such as Montgomery and Birmingham.

A UDAG was also used to rid the downtown of an eyesore. Dunlap sought an investor who would buy an abandoned theater in the downtown and convert it into a mixed-use commercial/office facility. The former theater had historical significance as the city's first theater and one of its oldest buildings, so Dunlap asked potential developers to maintain the marquee and other features of the theater as part of the renovation work. Once a developer was found who would buy the building and make the necessary financial commitment to renovate the old theater, Dunlap applied for a UDAG. The UDAG loan to the developer of $88,000 closed the financing gap that he faced and enticed him to undertake the project as the city wanted it. By taking a proactive position, the city was able to clean up an eyesore, save a historical structure, create twenty new jobs, generate $5,000 in new taxes annually, and have the UDAG of $88,000 plus interest owed to it by the developer.

The economic development director realized that the millions of dollars lent to the developers through the grants would be paid back to the city. The choice the city had, then, was either to spend the money on one-time projects, such as infrastructure improvements, or to recycle the money into a revolving loan fund (RLF) that could fund numerous other projects in the future. Even though no money was expected for several years, the city manager took the advice of the economic development director and submitted a proposal to the city council to establish an RLF from developer paybacks of the $10 million worth of federal grants. Figure 1 illustrates the elements of the Auburn RLF.

By the time the UDAG program was terminated by Congress in 1989, Auburn had a sizable amount of money invested in its RLF and was in a position to continue to create public-private partnerships based on the UDAG model. The RLF played a major part in Auburn's success in attracting jobs and creating investment because it gave Auburn a competitive advantage in economic development. By 1993, the city council had approved nine loans from the RLF totaling $785,000, and had issued two guarantees to banks for part of the equity needed by two small industrial projects. The private sector investment for these eleven projects exceeded $11.2 million and resulted in the creation of approximately 315 new jobs in the community.

All of the projects funded from the RLF have to meet the criteria set for the program. First, the money must be needed to make the project happen in Auburn. Some of the projects that were funded had sufficiently strong investors not to need the city's RLF to secure financing. However, the RLF has given the city the capability to recruit projects that could just as easily locate elsewhere. For example, a well-known restaurant chain was considering building in East Alabama and had its choice of several locations. Because Auburn was prepared to assist the company by making a $75,000 loan at a low interest rate to install utilities, the Auburn site was selected over an equally desirable site in another city.

Second, the project must produce jobs for low- and moderate-income residents and generate new taxes for the city. When some local investors considered purchasing a motel that was thirty years old and had not been maintained properly, they approached Economic Development Director Dunlap for assistance. They were interested in obtaining a franchise from a major chain but did not have sufficient equity to secure the necessary financing to remodel the motel to meet the standards of the franchiser. The city council authorized an interim loan of $75,000 for twelve months at an interest rate 2 percentage points below the prime rate that served as equity for the investors. In addition, Dunlap also arranged for the packaging of a 504 loan from the Small Business Administration. Dunlap's assistance resulted in the investors receiving the franchise which, in turn, was the key to the bank supplying the loan to remodel the motel. The nearly $2 million investment in this project produced sixteen new jobs and retained another thirty jobs. The increased taxes and fees from the investment for the city totalled $23,300.

Third, all loans are secured so that the city does not lose its RLF funds. When a major engineering company considered opening its southeastern headquarters in Auburn if local investors could be found to

FIGURE 1

City of Auburn Revolving Loan Fund

Program Components

Loan Guarantee Program

Term:	Match first mortgage
Rate:	Negotiable
Maximum guarantee:	Up to 30% of total loan for projects up to $200,000 in size
Structure:	Bank, 60%; bank, 30% (guaranteed); equity, 10%
Leverage ratio:	1:2.5
Job creation:	1 permanent job per $6,000
Equity:	10% required

Fixed Asset Loan Program—Direct Loan

Term:	Match first mortgage/life of asset
Rate:	Negotiable
Maximum amount:	$200,000 (based on project size of $500,000 or more)
Leverage:	1:2.5 (minimum)
Job creation:	1 permanent job per $6,000
Collateral:	Subordinate mortgage on fixed assets
Equity:	10% requirement, may be waived to 5% depending on viability of project

Infrastructure Development Program—Guarantee Program

Term:	Negotiable
Rate:	Negotiable
Maximum amount:	Not more than 51% of project cost
Leverage:	n/a
Job creation:	1 permanent job per $6,000

Working Capital Loan Program

Term:	1 to 3 years
Rate:	Negotiable
Maximum amount:	$25,000
Collateral:	Subordinate mortgage, contract assignment, receivable, personal guarantee, other

Interim Loan Program

Term:	1 year
Rate:	Negotiable
Maximum amount:	Funds available
Collateral:	Subordinate mortgage, personal guarantee, other

Housing Development Program (lot acquisition and construction financing)

Term:	As needed, generally short-term
Rate:	Negotiable
Maximum amount:	Unit construction cost
Collateral:	Unit and property

construct a building for the company to lease, Dunlap paired the company with two local investors who were interested in the project. The $50,000 loan from the RLF was secured by a subordinate mortgage on the real estate as well as personal guarantees of the investors. If borrowers have not had sizable personal worth, the city has required letters of credit from banks to secure the loans.

Meanwhile, Dunlap also developed a successful industrial recruitment record. Despite the very strong competition for industrial projects and Auburn's self-imposed restrictions, the city was still able to recruit eight industries that built plants in the Auburn industrial parks during the early 1990s. Some of these eight companies were new locations for firms headquartered in Indiana, Ohio, New York, and the United Kingdom. Two of the firms moved to Auburn from an adjoining city and another was a start-up that had grown to the point where it needed a larger facility. The city council's goal of bringing one new manufacturing company into the industrial park each year has been met since the city assumed responsibility for industrial development.

This second phase was important primarily because the city had to establish credibility for its role in economic development. Several relationships were especially important in this regard. First, the city's economic development effort needed the respect of the business community and, in particular, the Chamber of Commerce. The Chamber had provided the staff support for industrial recruitment for years and was an important ally in economic development. Many of the business leaders who had been involved with the IDB effort were skeptical of having this function located in City Hall and under the control of the city government. However, because the expertise of the economic development director was immediately beneficial to a number of prominent businessmen in the community, the business community supported the city's program.

Second, a major university has considerable economic influence in a community the size of Auburn. Even if it did not play an active role in economic development, the university would be influential simply because of the size of its budget and its payroll. The opportunity of the city staff to work with the president and executive vice president of Auburn University on the hotel/conference center, a project that originated with the university president, demonstrated the commitment and capability of the city in economic development. This project was the first in an economic development partnership that was developed between the university and the city. The key elements of that partnership will be explained in the next section.

Third, the city had to prove to itself that economic development was a function in which it should be involved. Prior to 1984, the city's role was to support the industrial development efforts of the IDB with limited funds. There were no city staff members assigned to economic development, so the decision in 1984 to assume responsibility for this function broke new ground. The success of the economic development director in securing the $10 million in UDAGs and other federal funds, the recruitment of new industries, and the assistance provided to the business community and the university in finding innovative ways to fund key projects gave assurance to the community's elected officials that the city could play an important role in economic development.

Phase 3: Creating Partnerships

One cornerstone of the city's economic development program has been a realization that it must be based on partnerships with other important constituencies in the community. A second cornerstone has been that the city's program is not narrowly confined to industrial recruitment but includes commercial and community development as well. Examples of the city's partnerships with the business community, the university, and state and federal agencies were given in the last section. The third phase of the city's involvement in economic development built on these same relationships but expanded them into innovative areas beyond industrial development. Several of the most important of these areas will be explored in this section.

City leaders realized that in order for the city to be attractive for economic development, attention must be given to infrastructure. Major projects were completed over the decade to improve the community's capacity for growth. For example, two new waste water treatment plants were built in an innovative privatization arrangement with a private company,[2] streets were built or widened and other existing ones were brought up to standard, new water-production and -distribution facilities were constructed, several parks were developed, and additional property was secured for industrial parks. In addition, the city constructed two downtown parking facilities that helped to stabilize the businesses located there and created a facade-improvement program that enticed the owners of downtown buildings to improve them.

In the city's broader view of economic development, several other projects were undertaken. For example, the city built a $2 million softball complex that has attracted thousands of softball players and their families to the community to play in tournaments and leagues. The city also initiated an affordable-housing program in partnership with banks, home builders, and community leaders. The city provides interest-free construction loans for builders chosen through competitive bids to build houses on city-owned lots, selects qualified low- and moderate-income buyers who are responsible for a $500 down payment, and commits a low-interest second mortgage to local banks that provide first-mortgage financing.

These economic development projects have created work for local businesses, homes for low- and moderate-income citizens, and significant tax revenue for the city. In addition, they have improved the quality of life in the community and encouraged other development. In the vicinity of the softball complex, several other large developments have now occurred, such as a new motel, convenience store, water theme park, and other businesses. In the neighborhoods where the city has constructed affordable housing, new private housing is being built for the first time in two decades.

Phase 4: Growing Industry

In industrial development, the competition among thousands of localities for the few limited manufacturing locations each year is severe. For the most part, cities the size of Auburn depend on state and other development agencies to bring industrial prospects to them. They may do some limited marketing of their communities through advertising and trade shows, but they cannot justify spending their resources on a broader effort when other agencies are already established to perform that function for them. Many communities, however, have something unique that they use in economic development. For example, port cities, such as Baltimore and Boston, have constructed popular waterfront tourist attractions while towns in the mountains, such as Gatlinburg, Tennessee, and Aspen, Colorado, have built their economies around their mountain locations. Auburn's advantage in economic development is that it has a major research university located there. The city's economic development director and others in leadership positions realized that a partnership with the university in economic development would be beneficial.

In 1985, Economic Development Director Dunlap suggested to state and university officials that a network of small-business incubators in Alabama was needed to encourage the development of home-grown industries. Working with the Economic Development Institute at the university, Dunlap was part of the team that researched and wrote a feasibility study to determine the applicability of the small-business incubator concept to the state. After the study recommended that the state fund three demonstration incubator programs, the governor agreed to use a portion of the state's Community Development Block Grant (CDBG) funds for this purpose. In 1987, the state selected Auburn as one of the sites for the incubator program and awarded $369,000 in CDBG funds to the city, which matched the state's funds. The initial 12,000 square foot building was completed in 1988 and the city council named the program the Auburn Center for Developing Industries (ACDI). A board of directors was established by the city council with three representatives of the city, including the city manager, the chairman of the IDB, and a city council member; three university officials, including the vice president for research, the dean of the College of Business, and the director of the Economic Development Institute; and one at-large member representing the business community.

Tenants of the ACDI are accepted for available space in the incubator after submitting an application that includes a business plan to the economic development director. After the director's initial review is completed, applicants have the opportunity to present their proposals to the ACDI board of directors, which has authority to accept or reject the applicant. The tenants in the program have several major advantages: (1) The Economic Development Department provides staff support to the businesses, such as word processing, photocopying, and telephone answering, on an as-needed basis at a reasonable cost; (2) the university offers technical assistance from the Colleges of Engineering and Business through a contract with ACDI; and, most important, (3) the rent for the space in the incubator is below market rates for the tenants. The city's rental rates are based on the cost to operate the facility and include no profit, since the city's motive is not to make money but to create jobs.

In 1989, the first tenant of the incubator occupied part of the available space, and within a short period of time the facility was at capacity. In 1992, the ACDI was expanded by 20,000 square feet and the two new buildings were immediately occupied by start-up industries. Interestingly, six of the seven tenants in the program in 1993 resulted from university research. Two were companies that secured the right to use patents generated through research at the university. One was a major corporation on the West Coast that was exploring the feasibility of using a new capacitor developed on campus in space research for electric automobiles. The incubator provided an excellent, low-overhead facility for the company to continue its research into the applicability of the adaptive use of this technology for commercial purposes. The second company was interested in producing a carbon-fiber material developed in the textile engineering laboratories of the university. The company believed that the material had widespread commercial applications if it could be manufactured and demonstrated to potential customers. The incubator provided the opportunity, at a reasonable cost, to develop this product.

The city's expectation in these and other incubator projects is that after the companies develop their products and their markets, they will build manufacturing facilities in the city's industrial parks. Prior to the availability of the incubator, products such as the capacitor and carbon fiber developed from research at the university left the Auburn area and the state. With the university's active involvement with the incubator, the likelihood of converting the university's research into jobs for the community and state was greatly enhanced.

By 1994, the companies in the ACDI employed approximately 150 people, and two of the companies were nearing graduation from the program. Executives of both were working with the economic development director to purchase land in the industrial park to build their own manufacturing facilities. The city council also committed to expand the incubator program by another 6,000 feet to accommodate a developing company moving to Auburn from Dallas. The company decided to move to Auburn after one of its suppliers, a tenant in ACDI, told the owner of the advantages of being in Auburn's incubator program.

A second example of the city using its partnership with the university was the construction of a multimillion-dollar research park. The city purchased 225 prime acres fronting on the interstate and hired a nationally known engineering firm to design an upscale research park with underground utilities, a small lake and recreation area, a jogging trail, and other amenities. The university was invited to build a 35,000 square foot research facility for its space power institute on the most desirable parcel of land in the park. The city and the university are planning to construct a technology transfer center in the park in the future that will build on the city's commitment to develop research as an industry.

Summary

The city of Auburn has used a number of weapons in its competition with other localities for investment and jobs. The UDAGs, the RLF, the various housing and other infrastructure programs, the small business incubator facility, and the research park are all examples of Auburn's efforts to be proactive in economic development.

There appear to be several key elements in the success of Auburn's program. First, the city developed partnerships with other organizations and groups. The university played an important role in the incubator, the research park, and the hotel/conference center. Local business interests invested in numerous projects through the Economic Development Department, such as the rehabilitation of the old theater in the downtown. The state and federal governments also were supportive of the city's program, both by funding projects brought to them and by bringing business prospects to the city.

Second, the city's approach to financing the economic development effort has been conservative. The use of the money recovered from the federal loans made to developers through the UDAG program has been subjected to the same scrutiny banks employ in making loans to commercial customers. Evidence of the city's conservative approach to safeguarding these funds is that no loans made by the city through the RLF have failed. The incubator facility is established on the basis that the rents collected pay for the expense of operating the facility. The cost of the city's economic development program is the amount budgeted each year for the Economic Development Department by the city council. It is clear that the revenue generated by the department since 1984 greatly exceeds the investment made by the city council in the economic development program.

Third, Auburn's program has been successful because of the strong support from the city's elected officials and the competency and initiative of the staff, particularly Economic Development Director Dunlap. The city council has been willing to support the various elements of the economic development program but only after a careful review of the potential costs and benefits. In addition, the staff of the Economic Development Department has been encouraged to be innovative in the ways it approaches problems and opportunities. This is evidenced both by the support it has received and by its successes.

This small city has developed a comprehensive economic development program over the past decade that has made it competitive for numerous projects. With the basics of the program in place in the form of the small-business incubator, the research park, the conventional industrial parks, the revolving loan fund, and a competent, innovative staff, Auburn is in a position to compete with much larger cities for investment and jobs over the next decade.

BESSEMER: A PAINFUL READJUSTMENT

Bessemer, Alabama, is located approximately fifteen miles from downtown Birmingham in the ridge and valley terrain that marks the southern foothills of the Appalachian Mountain Range.[3] This city of 32,000 occupies more than forty-five square miles, a large portion of which resulted from two major annexations in 1985 and 1986. Transportation needs are well served by two interstate highways, two major rail lines, and a local switching line that services some of the area's older heavy industries. The city also owns an airport that is used by general aviation and serves as a reliever airport for the larger airport in Birmingham.

The Early Years

Founded by industrialist Henry Debardeleben in 1886, the city was named in honor of Sir Henry Bessemer, the British inventor of the Bessemer process for making steel. Debardeleben purchased 4,000 acres of land along the tracks of the Alabama Great Southern Railroad and subdivided tracts of land for his city. He also built several blast furnaces for his coal and iron company and worked to attract industry and other development to his new town.

Almost immediately the city grew to 1,000 residents and within two years increased to 4,000. Promotion of the city was based almost entirely on its superior mineral wealth, including iron ore, coal, and limestone. All of the ingredients for making iron and steel were found in abundance within a narrow geographic region near Bessemer. The city developed as a significant industrial city that produced great wealth from iron and steel making and related heavy industrial manufacturing. Dependence on heavy industry and metals, however, left the city vulnerable to the swings of economic cycles. Recessions in 1893 and 1907 and the Great Depression of the 1930s produced economic turmoil for Bessemer, with high unemployment and limited purchasing power of its residents. After each downturn, however, the city was able to rebound with renewed vigor.

With the changes in the national economy in the late 1970s and early 1980s, and the lack of competitiveness of American steel companies, Bessemer's economy suffered greatly. Dependent for so long on the iron and steel mills that employed a high percentage of its residents, Bessemer now faced high unemployment (35 percent in 1983) and little prospect for recovery of the industries that had been responsible for the city's growth.

Changing Directions

With this dire situation facing them, Bessemer's elected officials decided that they had to take a fresh approach to economic development because they no longer could count on the industries that were the bases of the local economy since the city's founding 100 years earlier. It was at this time that the city created its Economic and Community Development Department and hired James Byram as as its first director. Byram had worked with Phillip Dunlap, the Auburn economic development director, for several years in Birmingham and had a reputation as an innovative and aggressive economic development professional. This department, working through the Industrial Development Board (IDB), was charged with developing a long-range program for diversifying the city's business base and strategically placing the city in a position where it would never again be totally dependent on one large employer or one industry for its economic well-being.

The IDB that existed when Byram arrived met infrequently, usually at the request of a local industry seeking to avail itself of tax-free financing for new equipment or building expansions. The IDB had no assets; its sole function was to enter into inducement agreements and to assume title to property financed through industrial development bonds. Through vesting title in the IDB, private firms could make such property exempt from state, county, and municipal ad valorem taxes.

The Chamber of Commerce also was active in the city but had realized little meaningful success in business development or industrial recruitment. Its leadership did not understand the potential use of government incentives or how public and private financial resources could complement each other in developing an assistance package for a prospective business. Mostly, however, the community had never had to be concerned with attracting new businesses or industries in the past because of the strong economic base provided by the iron and steel manufacturers.

The director of economic and community development was not given a budget but rather was instructed by the elected officials to raise funds through grants or other off-budget methods. Even though little in the way of financial resources was made available, the director was given a free hand in developing and implementing an economic development program. Fortunately for Bessemer, the city was eligible for the UDAG program and was an entitlement city in the CDBG program.

Grants Provide the Impetus

A turning point in Bessemer's economic history was the successful application the city filed with HUD to be classified as an entitlement city under the CDBG program. As an entitlement city, Bessemer was assured of an annual appropriation from HUD to use for projects benefiting low- and moderate-income citizens. The CDBG program also provided the funding the city used to establish its Economic and Community Development Department. It allowed the city to establish its economic development program in the face of an austere local budget that some elected officials believed could not be stretched far enough to fund a new function such as economic development.

While the CDBG funds were important to Bessemer's economic development effort, Byram's success with the UDAG program had a significant impact on the local economy. UDAG, a HUD program from

1977 to 1989, was intended to provide gap financing for projects in needy cities and urban counties that would otherwise not be constructed. The competitive program was based on the number of new jobs created, the ratio of private funds invested compared to the UDAG amount, and similar factors that would improve the economies of distressed cities. Byram, who had been successful in bringing millions of UDAG dollars to Birmingham while on the city staff there, began shortly after he arrived in Bessemer to develop applications to submit to HUD for funding.

In 1984, Byram submitted his first UDAG application for an industrial painting firm that needed a $110,000 low-interest loan from the city (with UDAG as the source of funds) to help purchase and renovate five vacant industrial buildings and acquire $200,000 worth of new capital equipment. The financing included a $125,000 loan for ten years from a local bank, a $125,000 Small Business Administration (SBA) 503 participation loan for a twenty-year term, a cash injection by the firm of $166,000, and the UDAG loan from the city for a twenty-year term. Byram's expertise in packaging the application with the diverse sources of funding for the company was the key to the creation of thirty permanent jobs and $7,035 in new taxes annually for the city. The project was especially important to Bessemer because it led to the rehabilitation of five industrial buildings that had been unoccupied in an industrial park for a number of years.

A second example of Byram's resourcefulness in utilizing various sources to assist a company in the creation of a viable funding package was the 1985 UDAG for a large *Fortune* 500 company that had allowed its Bessemer operations to deteriorate. With Byram's encouragement, the company agreed to seek funding through UDAG to replace obsolescent boilers and to install a condensing turbine that was capable of producing all the company's power needs at that location. The $360,530 UDAG proved to be the stimulus that led the company to invest $6.1 million in new facilities and equipment, raised through an industrial development bond issue sponsored by the Bessemer IDB. The city's role in seeking the UDAG and sponsoring the tax-free industrial development bond developed twenty new full-time jobs and more than $18,000 in direct new taxes for the city.

Before the UDAG program was terminated in 1989 by Congress, Byram had successfully packaged seven applications that brought $2.1 million to the city. All the funds were lent to businesses that created new jobs and taxes. In addition to the two UDAGs already mentioned, Bessemer received $420,000 to help build fifty-eight new low-income homes, $461,452 to renovate a historic downtown office building, $400,000 to a company that processes steel coils, $300,000 to a steel fabricator, and $70,000 to a minority-owned printing business. While these programs were significant in helping the Bessemer economy to recover, Bessemer's reuse of the funds became even more important to the long-term economic health of the community.

Bessemer decided to create a revolving loan fund through its IDB utilizing several sources of funds. Paybacks from the UDAGs were designated to be placed in the RLF. Furthermore, part of the city's CDBG funds was used to help in the capitalization of the RLF. Byram was also able to convince the elected officials to donate to the IDB two vacant parcels of land owned by the city and develop them as industrial parks. The appraised value of the land was included on the IDB's financial statement. The RLF provided the financial basis for the creation of Bessemer's industrial lease program.

Developing an Industrial Lease Program

As is often the case with innovation, the development of the Bessemer industrial lease program resulted from addressing an opportunity. A small out-of-state company, specializing in servicing equipment for the mining industry, was searching for a site to lease in an adjoining city. A local citizen heard about the company's efforts and informed the Bessemer Economic and Community Development Department staff of it. Because Bessemer was as close to the coal mines as the other city, the staff contacted the company and invited its officials to visit Bessemer. The type and size of facility needed by the company was not readily available in Bessemer, so, in order to be competitive with the other city, the staff proposed that the IDB construct a building for the company on land owned by the IDB in one of the city's industrial parks.

During the company's visit to Bessemer, Byram informed the prospect of the IDB's offer to build and lease a 6,200 square foot metal building for the company at a favorable rent. The IDB had accrued enough cash from UDAG paybacks and miscellaneous fees to pay for the building. The prospect selected a site in the industrial park and left the construction details to the IDB staff. After a period of negotiation between the city and the company, a lease was executed that provided for a rent of $1,200 per month for a building that cost the IDB $110,000 to construct. The company was given an option to purchase the property from the IDB for $10,000 per acre for the two acres on which the building was placed plus the amortized amount of $110,000 at 9 percent over thirty years at the date of sale.

The IDB staff calculated the rent payment to approximate a fifteen-year payback, which was the maximum time a commercial bank would lend for industrial real estate. The rent figure was below market rate because the IDB did not have to include the cost of the land or any developer's profit, nor did it have to pay ad valorem taxes. The primary advantage to the IDB was that it located the company in Bessemer and created new jobs in a community that was suffering from high unemployment. It was also a successful business arrangement for the IDB, however, which had its money invested in real estate that was paying a return of 9 percent. Even if the company failed, the IDB still owned a valuable asset. This arrangement also offered the company some credit toward eventual ownership based on the amount of rent paid to the IDB. This proved to be a strong incentive to the company since it desired eventually to own the building.

This first building lease was entered into by the company and the IDB in October 1987. In 1989, Bessemer had the opportunity to build a second building and lease it to an industry looking for a site in the South. This prospect was a Canadian company that manufactured polystyrene patterns for foundries. The IDB offered to construct an industrial building at a cost of $453,000 and lease it to the company for an initial three-year term. This proposal enabled Bessemer to prevail over the incentive packages offered to the prospect by several other communities competing for this project.

By this time, the IDB's portfolio included a number of other successful loans, including the first industrial building free of debt. The staff invited local banks to lend the IDB the funds necessary to construct this second industrial building. After reviewing the financial statements of the Canadian company, a bank agreed to lend the amount of the construction cost to the IDB on a three-year note that was concurrent with the term of the lease between the IDB and the company. The lease was later extended for an additional five years.

Realizing the economic development potential of this type of incentive program and the capital formation capability it offered to the IDB, the staff began to market this concept to selected new and expanding small businesses that were in need of industrial space. From 1987, when the first building lease project was done, until early 1994, the IDB constructed and leased eight industrial facilities costing more than $1.6 million. Three of the eight companies required additions to be constructed to handle increased business. The eight tenants in the buildings owned by the IDB employ nearly 100 people.

Table 1 compares the values of selected assets generated by the IDB over a four-year period. The results, taken from the IDB's annual audits, illustrate the growth of the IDB's holdings, exclusive of any federal grant paybacks. For example, rental income to the IDB increased from $16,900

TABLE 1

Four-year audit comparison of selected unrestricted assets
for Bessemer Industrial Development Board, by year

	1989	1990	1991	1992
Fixed assets*	636,816	1,300,561	1,314,720	1,699,182
Total assets	2,126,923	2,794,577	3,148,784	3,502,632
Fund equity	1,732,173	2,205,153	2,453,716	2,507,992
Retained earnings	1,020,534	1,143,114	1,391,677	1,445,953
Notes payable	344,584	335,925	660,735	644,349
Rental income	16,900	95,850	163,900	216,750

*Less accumulated depreciation

Source: Jim Byram, "Preservation of Capital as a Tool in Economic Development," thesis, University of Oklahoma, 1993.

in 1989 to $216,750 in 1992. All eight leases performed satisfactorily and half have been renewed periodically at higher rental rates. By 1993, rental revenue exceeded debt service by more than $10,000 per month. The Bessemer IDB has become a successful real estate investor for the purpose of bringing jobs into the community.

The Bessemer program offers many attractive incentives for industries. The most obvious incentive for an industry is its ability to occupy a new customized industrial building with no out-of-pocket costs. Available cash may be retained for working capital or the purchase of equipment, machinery, or inventory. If the company needs to seek financing from a lender for any of these items, it is not burdened with a large long-term liability.

Another incentive is the purchase option that amortizes a portion of each rent payment toward eventual ownership. For example, a business might be given an option to purchase a building that costs $100,000 to construct based on a thirty-year amortization schedule at a 10 percent interest rate. The IDB may negotiate an initial monthly rent of $1,200, which is more than adequate to amortize a fifteen-year bank loan, and then increase the rental rate when the lease is renewed. The IDB has used the consumer price index as the basis for increases in lease rates. Within a 15-year period, the IDB would satisfy all debt on the structure and would be sole owner of the building. However, the company could exercise its option to purchase the building at any time during the lease period. If the company exercised its option to purchase after fifteen years, the IDB would have made a profit on the building for fifteen years. The IDB is able to sell the land for the original cost per acre and the building for an agreed upon amount after credit is given the company for its lease payments under the lease purchase arrangement. This agreement is beneficial to the company because it can buy the property at a price that does not include appreciation in value over the years of the lease. The advantage to Bessemer is that the company has a vested interest in the building and will likely remain in the city.

Summing It Up

While the Economic and Community Development Department has utilized the industrial lease program to achieve excellent results, it has also employed numerous other, more traditional, recruitment tools to attract investment and create jobs in Bessemer. The hand of Jim Byram and his staff members can be seen in every major project undertaken in Bessemer over the past nine years. Through their innovative approach to economic development, they have placed the city in a superior position when it has had to compete with other cities for projects. The IDB's competitiveness has resulted in an outstanding record for the city since Byram arrived in 1984:

1. The IDB has targeted distribution centers for recruitment to Bessemer that serve Alabama and the Southeast and that would normally be located in Birmingham, the largest city in the state. For example, the industrial parks along the interstate serving Bessemer have provided warehouse space for companies such as Big B Drugs (500,000 square feet), Piggly-Wiggly grocery chain (530,000 square feet), Baxter medical and hospital supplies (110,000 square feet), Stuart Hall paper products (110,000 square feet), and James River Paper Company (400,000 square feet).

2. A resurgence in the area's steel industry has been made possible by the U.S. Steel Corporation's commitment to modernize its older factory located in Bessemer. As a result, the IDB has targeted a diverse group of industries that have special niches in the steel market. Companies that process, fabricate, treat, manufacture, or distribute steel products have helped to re-employ some of the area's displaced steel workers. All of these new-generation steel- and metal-industry companies are small in comparison to the large corporations of previous decades. Most of the new companies employ between ten and seventy-five workers rather that the thousands employed by the old steel works. All have narrowly defined markets in which they fill a special need.

3. More than forty new industrial and warehouse companies have located in Bessemer since the Economic and Community Development Department was formed. Another dozen companies have been helped by the IDB staff to expand over this same period. Evidence of this expanding sector of the local economy is that business license applications with the city of Bessemer have increased dramatically. In 1985, the companies buying business licenses in the industrial category reported combined sales of $103 million; by 1991, the figure had increased to over $300 million.

4. The unemployment rate for Bessemer fell from 35 percent in 1984 to less than 10 percent in the early 1990s. Furthermore, the labor force grew from 12,990 to 15,230 in 1991, which means that the growth in jobs has been even better than the recent rate of unemployment might indicate. Total employment increased over this period by 3,680 jobs.

Bessemer is a city that had failed to be competitive in economic development over the decades because of its strong reliance on one major industry. However, after that industry declined and unemployment soared, community leaders were wise enough to develop a strategy to rejuvenate the city's economy. Its first step was to establish an Economic and Community Development Department and hire a competent professional who brought millions of dollars in grants into the city. Most important, the IDB has been able to create a strong portfolio of real estate holdings through its willingness to construct buildings for industrial prospects.

CONCLUSION

Auburn and Bessemer have several things in common in the way they have built their economic development programs over the past decade. First, both have hired competent and innovative professionals to develop programs where none existed prior to their arrivals. Second, Auburn and Bessemer were able to utilize federal and state programs effectively to generate significant amounts of cash for their programs. Third, both cities have taken conservative approaches that recognize the financial gaps that industries have in starting new ventures and have offered assistance in those areas. For example, Auburn's incubator assists start-up companies to develop with below-market rents, pooled secretarial help, and technical consulting available from the university. Bessemer's industrial lease program helps industries to locate in new buildings at little or no initial capital outlay and allows them to preserve their capital for other needs, such as purchases of equipment or materials.

Through their innovative approaches to economic development, both cities have positioned themselves to compete with the thousands of other localities that also want the limited new investment and jobs created each year in this country.

NOTES

1. Larry D. Terry, "Why We Should Abandon the Misconceived Quest to Reconcile Public Entrepreneurship with Democracy," *Public Administration Review* 53, no. 4 (July/August 1993): 393–95; Carl J. Bellone and George Frederick Goerl, "In Defense of Civic-Regarding Entrepreneurship or Helping Wolves to Promote Good Citizenship," *Public Administration Review* 53, no. 4 (July/August 1993): 396–98.

2. John G. Heilman and Gerald W. Johnson, *The Politics and Economics of Privatization* (Tuscaloosa, Ala: University of Alabama Press, 1992), 62–80.

3. This case study relies heavily on Jim Byram, "Preservation of Capital as a Tool in Economic Development," thesis, Economic Development Institute, University of Oklahoma, 1993.

4 The States as Competitors

The success of local governments in economic development is largely dependent on the support they receive from their state governments. States have played an important role in economic development since the founding of this country. The focus on states' roles over the past decade has been on the magnitude of the incentives states are willing to offer to attract companies to communities within their borders. The increased competition in recent years has become so acute that many people in economic development are calling for a truce among the states. For example, Illinois Governor Jim Edgar proposed in 1993 that the National Governors' Association (NGA) develop a strategy on incentives that would eliminate the competition among states.[1] While no action was taken immediately, other governors acknowledged the need for a cooperative approach to the problem of the escalating war of incentives. At Governor Edgar's urging, the NGA, meeting in Tulsa in August 1993, passed a resolution that stated: "States will always be in competition with each other for business investments. However, this competition should not be characterized by how much direct assistance a state can provide to individual companies." The nation's governors called on states to adopt incentives, such as worker training, that benefited entire communities and not individual companies.[2]

States are involved in local economic development in numerous other ways beyond granting tax breaks and other incentives. The efforts of states to create jobs or investment are done in concert with some local entity, such as a city government. It would be highly unusual, and probably unsuccessful, for a state development agency to attempt to place an industry in a community without consulting community leaders. Local leaders have some control over the use of land through zoning in their communities for industrial or commercial purposes, so they would have to be consulted before any commitments were made by the state.

The efforts of state governments are especially important to small cities and rural counties that do not have adequate resources to attract economic development on their own. Larger cities and counties have resources sufficient to compete with other localities, and, in many states, they view the state agency simply as support for their efforts. An example of a state's role in aiding rural communities was the hotly contested competition for the location of a Canadian steel mill with 400 jobs in 1993. Kentucky outbid offers from Pennsylvania and Ohio to land the plant. The company was considering rural or small-town locations in all three states. Gary Enos, commenting on the offers of all three states, said, "All three offers were driven primarily by state governments, with the localities playing a secondary role."[3]

It is a normal practice of state development agencies to provide training for officials in small cities and rural areas in economic development. Some states have teams of state employees that inspect the readiness of localities for industrial recruitment and provide advice to local officials on infrastructure needs as well as prompting them on the answers they must give if the state brings a prospect to them. As noted in chapter 2, some states encourage localities to construct speculative buildings and offer other incentives to make them "prepared for industry."

Active participation of local leaders in economic development is crucial to the success of state development efforts. A new business in any community wants to be assured that it has the support of local governmental leaders, and usually insists on having that support prior to committing to locate in the community. In effect, then, the state and local economic development efforts need to be closely coordinated if they are to be successful.

THE IMPORTANCE OF ADEQUATE INFRASTRUCTURE

One major role that states have in economic development is providing adequate infrastructure, such as transportation facilities, or assisting local governments in the construction of needed facilities, such as water and sewage plants.

Surveys of industries considering the construction of new manufacturing facilities indicate that transportation is usually among the most important factors in choosing a location. It is essential for a manufacturer to receive raw materials from its suppliers and to ship its finished products to its customers in a cost-effective manner. In order to accomplish this, companies must have access to adequate transportation facilities. All states are responsible for the construction of major highways, such as interstates, that link cities and towns. They also have the ability to widen roads to accommodate the heavier traffic generated by a new industry. For example, in its commitments to the Canadian steel company it recruited for rural Gallatin County in 1993, Kentucky agreed to widen a major highway in the county that would serve the industry.[4]

Other infrastructure must also be adequate to serve the needs of the industry. Local governments have to be able to demonstrate that they have sufficient capacity and quality of water and sewage facilities to accommodate the new development. In the Kentucky case, the state committed to make a $4 million loan to the local water and sewer authority to upgrade its facilities to handle the water and sewer needs of the industry.[5] This type of aid is not unusual from a state government, especially in rural areas where resources to build the necessary infrastructure are often lacking.

EDUCATION'S IMPORTANCE IN ECONOMIC DEVELOPMENT

States generally have primary responsibility in the area of education from kindergarten through research universities. With the major changes in the nation's economy, education is viewed as an extremely important element in making an area attractive to high-technology industries. Schools are not only important for the quality of the graduates they produce to work in industry, but they must be of high enough quality to entice executives with children to move into the community. Most industries relocate several key managers to a new plant site and oftentimes include them as part of the selection team that reviews the various locations under consideration. The opinions of the managers who are to be relocated generally play a considerable role in the final site selection, and substandard local schools may be the reason a community is not selected.

It is not coincidental that the growth of many high-tech industries in the United States has taken place close to major universities, as explained in chapter 2. Numerous examples are available, such as the industrial growth around the Research Triangle in North Carolina, near Harvard University and the Massachusetts Institute of Technology in Massachusetts, and in the Silicon Valley near Stanford University in California.

THE DEBATE OVER INCENTIVES STATES OFFER

Some of the most widely used incentives offered by states to lure industries include tax-free financing, property tax breaks, construction of infrastructure, site development grants, training for workers, and low cost (and sometimes free) land in fully served industrial parks. While some states are willing to offer more incentives than others, all states are now actively in competition with each other for new industry. In recent years there has been an escalation in the value of the incentives states have offered for industrial site locations, as mentioned previously. Calls for an end to the incentive battles, such as the one from Governor Edgar, have not been heeded by states anxious for quality jobs.

Numerous studies over the years have questioned the value of incentives in the attraction of industry. Generally, these studies have argued that other factors, such as the community's "quality of life" or proximity to markets, play a much greater role than do financial incentives in the decision making of major corporations in choosing a site.

The questionable value of incentives in attracting new manufacturing firms to communities was confirmed in a survey completed by a national real estate consulting firm in 1993. Deloitte & Touche interviewed 150 corporate real estate executives and 658 state and local economic developers in an effort to determine the value both groups place on incentives. The corporate executives ranked incentives fourteenth out of seventeen choices in importance to them when they made relocation or expansion decisions. The top five factors in making location decisions were all related to a community's inherent qualities: real estate costs, labor force issues, transportation, availability of facilities and/or property, and access to market. When the corporate executives were asked how important incentives were to them in making locational choices, 28 percent said "very important," 26 percent "moderately important," 20 percent "somewhat important," 23 percent "not a factor," and only 3 percent said they were "critical."[6]

The economic developers viewed incentives as playing a more important role in locational decisions than did the corporate executives. Forty-two percent said incentives were "very important," 22 percent "moderately important," 20 percent "critical," 12 percent "somewhat important," and only 4 percent said they were "not a factor."[7] The economic developers rated the importance of various incentives in the following order:

1. Infrastructure improvement
2. Property tax abatement

3. Regulatory flexibility
4. Tax credits
5. Utility rate incentives
6. Land or facility cost write-down
7. Public finance/grants
8. Enterprise zone
9. Subsidized training
10. Employee relocation assistance[8]

Sixty-three percent of the economic developers also reported that they noticed an increase compared to three years ago in the level of incentives that companies were seeking from them as a condition of locating in their communities. Mark Klender reports:

> The bottom line is that competition between jurisdictions to attract business is fierce right now, especially given the slow national economy. . . .
>
> [C]ompanies are seeking more incentives than they did three years ago, reflecting the publicity that big incentives have received and the fact that economic development right now is decidedly a buyer's market.[9]

The corporate executives and the public economic developers agreed that incentives are most important in their role as "tie-breakers" in the final stages of the locational process. After a company has reduced its choices of communities to three to five, and all have the inherent qualities that are most important to the corporation, then an especially strong incentive package may serve as the factor that a company relies on to make a choice.[10]

A site-selection consultant advised his corporate clients: "The long-term viability of a location is most important. If there are three or four locations that are near optimal, then let incentives determine the final choice. But never sacrifice or trade off any major criteria for the sake of a short-term gain in incentives."[11]

It is important to note, however, that there is little or nothing a state or community can do to affect its proximity to a company's market or to improve its quality of life during the relatively short time a company is conducting its search for a new site. On the other hand, incentives are something that are within the power of the state to control. State legislatures have the authority to grant tax abatements, establish training programs, build infrastructure, and provide other incentives through legislation. Legislators obviously believe that these incentives bring jobs to their states and to their constituents, so they are anxious to appear to be doing all they can to promote economic development.

Historically, this has been more the case in some states than in others. Southern states hungry for industrial development have been the leaders in offering incentives to industries to locate there. For example, the first use of industrial development bonds was by Mississippi in 1936. However, in recent years, states in the North, Midwest, and West have realized the need to compete as they have lost hundreds of thousands of high-paying jobs to Sun Belt states. California has seen an exodus of companies over the past decade partly because of the perceived antibusiness policies of the state government.[12] One publication noted that California

> was a national leader in preserving endangered species, protecting coastlines, new restrictions on industry to clean air, high Workers' Compensation costs and business taxes, tax policies (like unitary treatment of corporate income) considered a barrier by many firms, and lethargy in acting on government permits required to build or expand facilities.[13]

As California leaders realized that they were losing their industrial base to other states that did not have policies that made it expensive to do business, they responded:

> The turnaround in state policies has been rapid and dramatic. Workers' Compensation has been reformed with lower rates a result. Unitary taxes are essentially a thing of the past. New tax concessions for development were passed last year. State and local officials are courting business more aggressively. Both parties in the Legislature appear eager to do more.[14]

In Massachusetts, the state legislature eliminated a requirement that corporations disclose their tax payments because it was perceived as contributing to an "antibusiness atmosphere." The head of a citizens' tax group responded by claiming that "business said 'jump' and 102 legislators said, 'how high?' "[15]

CONCLUSION

It is not possible to discuss local economic development without understanding the extremely important roles played by state governments. Under the doctrine of Dillon's Rule, local governments are the creations of state governments and have only those powers granted to them under state law. Therefore, even the ability of local governments to engage in economic development is controlled by the states. If a state legislature determines that local governments should restrict their activities to the provision of traditional services, then local governments have no authority to issue industrial development bonds, build industrial parks, or engage in any other economic development activity.

As can be seen by the evidence presented in this chapter, state governments are very active players in economic development. Not only do they provide numerous weapons to local governments, but they have a wide-ranging list of incentives they employ to encourage development, particularly industrial development. Nowhere is the concept of competitive governments more obvious than among states competing for new industries. However, with the possible exceptions of foreign industries or new-products manufacturing, most industrial locations do not create more jobs in the national economy. Industries moving from one state to another may create jobs in the state where the new plant is built, but a similar or greater number of jobs are lost in the state from which the industry moved.

One of the most highly publicized cases of industrial competition among states in recent years was the decision by Mercedes-Benz to locate a new manufacturing plant in the United States in 1993. There were months of speculation in the press with respect to where the German auto maker would manufacture its new four-wheel-drive utility vehicle. The following chapter presents a case study of the successful effort made by the state of Alabama to land the Mercedes-Benz project and the manner in which the governor informed the public of the extent of the cost to the state of acquiring the Mercedes-Benz plant. The monetary value of the incentive package offered by Alabama exceeded any prior package by a state to locate a new industry. The initial euphoric reaction within Alabama was dimmed by a steady stream of revelations of the commitments made by the governor and his industry-seeking team.

NOTES

1. Gary Enos, "Big Breaks Lure Plant to Ky.," *City and State*, 21 June–4 July 1993, 1 and 22.
2. Gary Kerr, "Governors Want to Ease Bidding Wars," *Montgomery Advertiser*, 17 September 1993, 2B.
3. Enos, 22.
4. Ibid.
5. Ibid.

6. Mark Klender, "Public Incentives," *Business Facilities*, August 1993, 24.

7. Ibid., 25.

8. Ibid.

9. Ibid., 23.

10. Ibid., 24.

11. Nancy Bader, "Incentives: The Name of the Game," *Area Development*, September 1993, 46.

12. "Economic Development Competition," *State Policy Reports* 12, no. 1 (January 1993), 12.

13. Ibid.

14. Ibid.

15. Ibid., 13.

5 Alabama Attracts Mercedes-Benz

The German auto maker Mercedes-Benz announced in April 1993 that it was planning to build its first manufacturing facility in the United States and would be searching for a site over the next several months. Its German rival BMW already had a plant under construction in South Carolina to be ready in 1995. The press speculated that the reasons Mercedes-Benz was looking to the United States as a site for building its new four-wheel-drive utility vehicle were the weakness of the dollar and the soaring cost of labor in Germany.[1]

The Mercedes announcement sparked an intense competition among states. The media reported that more than thirty states submitted sites to Mercedes-Benz Project, Inc., a subsidiary based in Chicago for the sole purpose of handling the site selection. Early speculation was that the company would select North Carolina or South Carolina because a subsidiary of Mercedes has three existing plants in North Carolina. Eventually Mercedes reportedly narrowed its potential sites to a handful of southern states—the Carolinas, Georgia, Tennessee, Mississippi, and Alabama.

THE COMPETITION BEGINS

During the several months leading to an announcement by Mercedes of its choice for a site to build its plant, the states that were involved as finalists engaged in a fierce battle to offer incentive packages that were superior to their competitors. The North Carolina legislature approved the construction of a $35 million Advanced Automotive Technology Center dubbed "Mercedes University" by the press. The center's sole purpose was to train auto workers for the Mercedes plant, and it would not be built if Mercedes did not locate in North Carolina.[2] North Carolina also offered $20 million in land, $8 million in training programs, and $15 million for infrastructure improvements leading to the site and on the site. Other long-term tax incentives reportedly were worth tens of millions of dollars.[3] The other states in the bidding war made similar offers to the North Carolina offer. For example, Georgia offered to provide the land for the project, lend Mercedes $300,000 at a low interest rate, build a training center and train the workers to Mercedes' specifications, improve the highway leading to the site from two interstate highways, and place a "Distance Learning Center" in the plant.[4]

During June, July, and August of 1993, the governors of South Carolina, Tennessee, Georgia, North Carolina, and Alabama visited Mercedes officials in Germany. Alabama's governor made two announced trips during this time. Prior to the second trip, he told the press that Alabama had made the "so-called short list" for the Mercedes project. South Carolina's governor was in Germany for a meeting with Mercedes executives the day before the Alabama governor was there. Secrecy shrouded the meetings. The Associated Press noted: "[C]onfirming details about meetings with Mercedes officials can be like trying to prove an Elvis siting[sic]."[5]

In late August 1993, the governor of Alabama called the state legislature into special session to consider a package of incentives to offer Mercedes. The centerpiece of the incentive package was a new tax-break law to lure companies to the state. It was modeled after Kentucky legislation that created the Kentucky Rural Economic Development Authority (KREDA) four years earlier. Kentucky economic development officials claimed that KREDA was responsible for enticing seventy new companies and 12,000 jobs to the state over the four years since its passage.[6]

The incentives approved by the Alabama legislature in its special session called by the governor were probably the most generous and innovative ever offered a company by a state government. The final vote on the legislation authorizing the incentives was nearly unanimous. The vote served as a strong indicator of the importance the legislators ascribe to economic development. The governor proclaimed after the legislation was passed: "We have won an important victory in bringing jobs to Alabama."[7]

The package that was offered to Mercedes by Alabama was valued at $253,328,000 by the Alabama Development Office, the agency primarily responsible for recruiting the company to the state. The state and several local governments committed to infrastructure improvements valued at $77.5 million. They included such projects as water, gas, and sewer line extensions to the site; electrical system improvements; and new roads, including a new interchange on the interstate highway near the site. The state and local governments also offered $92,150,000 of incentives for site development, including purchase and development of the site, at a cost of $30 million; a rail extension; and the construction of a training college/center valued at $30 million.

As mentioned, several city and county governments participated with the state in offering commitments to the company if it located in Alabama. For example, the Associated Press reported the action of the City Council of Tuscaloosa, Alabama, on the Mercedes incentive package:

> The Tuscaloosa City Council upped the ante $30 million Tuesday in the high-stakes bidding war for a Mercedes-Benz plant.
>
> The City Council voted unanimously to spend up to $30 million to buy and develop a 1,000 acre site near Vance, 19 miles east of Tuscaloosa.
>
> The resolution approved by the City Council provides that the Tuscaloosa County Industrial Development Authority would sell the site to Mercedes-Benz for $100.[8]

Other incentives included waiving sales and use taxes on equipment and material purchased during construction of the facility as well as on the machinery and equipment bought to be used in the manufacturing process. Through the Economic Development Partnership, an organization funded by thirty-three corporations to promote Alabama, the private sector also committed $15 million to the incentive package.

The critical provisions of the Alabama law that was passed to entice Mercedes were based on the Kentucky KREDA legislation. The company could use the money that it would normally pay to the state in corporate income taxes for debt service on its manufacturing facility. Furthermore, the company could withhold 5 percent of the wages and salaries of its employees and use it for debt service as well. The state, in turn, would then deduct the amount taken from the employees by the company from the amount owed the state in income taxes. The Associated Press stated: "That would be the equivalent of letting a person deduct all monthly home payments—principal and interest—from personal state income tax as an incentive to move to the state."[9] In essence, then, the state and local governments were paying for the total capital cost of the auto maker building a plant in the United States.

The *Wall Street Journal* commented on Alabama's incentive package:

> But what has really stunned economic development experts throughout the South is a package of tax breaks, valued at more than $300 million, that would, among other things, allow Mercedes to pay off its plant with the money it would have spent on state income taxes. "Apparently those people are buying and paying for the whole building," says J. Mac Holladay, who has directed economic development efforts of South Carolina and Mississippi, and was involved in Georgia's bid for the plant. "This steps over the line for the South."[10]

Speculation in the news media was widespread during the two weeks prior to the Mercedes announcement. The following is a sampling of newspaper headlines from the weeks before the announcement:

> "Report: North Carolina to get Mercedes plant"
>
> "Mississippi struck from Mercedes list"
>
> "Alabama reported as a Mercedes finalist"
>
> "[Tennessee Governor] McWherter not optimistic on Benz plant"
>
> "Rumors: Mercedes steering for Alabama"
>
> "Mercedes interested in Athens (Georgia) site"
>
> "Mercedes reportedly considering site near Charleston"

The week prior to the date the company announced its selection, the governors of North Carolina, South Carolina, Tennessee, and Georgia were invited to Germany by Chancellor Helmut Kohl to discuss the Mercedes project. The governor of Alabama was not invited, which sent mixed signals to those trying to second-guess the company. It implied either that Mercedes officials were planning to tell the governors of the losing states the bad news in person or that the company had already eliminated Alabama so it was not included in any further discussions. Speculation was heightened when the governor of North Carolina cancelled his plans to fly to Germany shortly before the meeting was to take place. Mercedes officials kept the suspense at a high level when they disclosed, the day before the announcement, that they would fly auto writers from Detroit to the chosen site for a news conference. The media widely reported that three sites were in final consideration by the company: Mebane, North Carolina; Summerville, South Carolina; and Vance, Alabama. The *Washington Post* reported that the plant would go to North Carolina, while the *Wall Street Journal* predicted that Mercedes would choose Alabama.

Finally, on 29 September, Mercedes notified the Alabama governor that it would hold its press conference in Tuscaloosa the next day to announce that Mercedes was coming to Alabama. Interestingly, at the press conference, the role of the incentives was downplayed by Mercedes:

> "Ours was a hard decision but, in the end, a clear one," said Mercedes-Benz Chairman Helmut Werner, making his first visit to Tuscaloosa for Thursday's news conference at the University of Alabama.
>
> Following a six-month search, Mr. Warner said, Mercedes-Benz' top executives became convinced that the state's work force, transportation network, the university environment in Tuscaloosa, as well as the state's business vitality and favorable "quality of life" made Alabama the best choice.
>
> Various incentive packages offered by states vying for the plant were quite similar and were not a decisive factor in the decision.[11]

The immediate reaction to the announcement was one of pride and jubilation within the state:

> Alabama officials were giddy over the announcement, which paired a luxury car company with one of the nation's poorest states, a place known more for racial unrest and football than for stylish, global industry.
>
> "This, my friends, is a new day for Alabama, a day when we move to the forefront of economic development," said Gov. Jim Folsom.[12]

A giant Mercedes logo was installed by anonymous corporate donors at a cost of $75,000 at Legion Field in Birmingham in time for a nationally televised University of Alabama football game.[13] Additionally, economic development marketers immediately seized the opportunity to promote Alabama because of the Mercedes decision. The Economic Development Partnership placed full-page advertisements in the *Wall Street Journal*, London's *Financial Times*, and Frankfurt's *Handelsblatt*. The Partnership announced that it was changing its $1.8 million annual marketing strategy to capitalize on the Mercedes location story. In addition, Mercedes officials joined representatives of the Partnership in media visits with editorial boards nationwide.[14]

Some in the national media appeared shocked by the Mercedes decision to locate in Alabama. The *Wall Street Journal* described Alabama's historical problems in race relations, education, and economic development and stated that "Alabama has remained woefully behind."[15] A *Washington Post* columnist, who was widely quoted in the Alabama media, wrote:

> Mercedes may have blundered this time by announcing last week it will build a plant in Alabama. Think about this: You're ready to pop for $85,000 on a car. You look in the glove compartment, and see a sign that says, "This Mercedes was handcrafted by Vernon 'Fishhead' Clampett, Tuscaloosa. That'll be 85 big ones." I don't think so. Maybe they'll sell in Alabama. But what about those numerical combination door locks? This is calculus in Alabama. The whole state could be locked out of their 500SELs with those ROOOLLL-TIDE vanity plates.
>
> When someone mentions "Mercedes," I just don't expect "Alabama." It doesn't feel right.[16]

An editor of the *Atlanta Journal* claimed that the Mercedes offer from Alabama reflected the willingness of Alabama to sacrifice "anything —natural resources, clean air and water, their economic future—for something of value now." He stated further that the "dramatic giveaway . . . has shocked public officials into a reassessment of the game of corporate tax giveaways."[17] The head of the Georgia Department of Industry, Trade and Tourism was quoted as saying that Georgia would not accept the Mercedes plant under the terms offered by Alabama because of the negative effect it would have on existing industries.

FROM VICTORY TO PUBLIC RELATIONS NIGHTMARE

Some of the early euphoria in the state over the Mercedes announcement began to fade after the director of the Alabama Development Office (ADO) urged city, county, and educational institutions in the state to buy or lease Mercedes automobiles because "we need to express our support to this company, our gratitude, our appreciation."[18] The governor and the ADO director began immediately driving "loaner cars" from Mercedes. The *Birmingham News* editorialized:

> We can appreciate everybody's enthusiasm about the legendary but struggling German automaker deciding to build its new sport vehicle in Alabama. . . .
>
> But this is pandering. This is groveling. This is downright pathetic. This is why people make fun of Alabama.
>
> Is our state such an unlikable place that we have to continue buying the good will of Mercedes-Benz? And isn't all this Mercedes overkill an insult to every company that was creating jobs and economic growth in Alabama before the German automaker came along?[19]

The governor decided to tour the General Motors plant in Decatur, Alabama, "to smooth ruffled feathers" over the ADO director's suggestion for state and local agencies to buy Mercedes sport utility vehicles. The governor traveled to the General Motors plant, which employs more than 3,500 people, in a Chevrolet. However, within days it was revealed that the Alabama recruiting team had committed to purchasing 2,500 of the new sport utility vehicles from Mercedes over a ten-year period as part of the incentive package. The ADO director's recommendation that state agencies, local governments, and educational institutions purchase Mercedes sports utility vehicles was in response to the commitment made by the state in its incentive package to Mercedes.

The value of the commitment to purchase the 2,500 sport vehicles was placed at $75 million and was not included in the analysis released to the public of the costs and benefits to the state of the bid to attract Mercedes. The governor faced an additional problem in making good on his commitment to Mercedes—a state law passed in 1976 requires state and local agencies to purchase vehicles exclusively from authorized General Motors, Ford, Chrysler, and American Motors dealers.

When pressed about this aspect of the incentive package, the governor stated that the whole deal depended on the state's commitment to buy the 2,500 vehicles: "Gov. Jim Folsom, Jr. said Monday that Alabama offered to buy 2,500 of Mercedes-Benz's new sport utility vehicles over the next decade because the state would have lost the German automaker's plant if it hadn't."[20] The governor's decision to offer to purchase the 2,500 vehicles was based on "very reliable information" that South Carolina and North Carolina had agreed to purchase 2,000 of the vehicles from Mercedes as part of their commitment packages. A spokesman for South Carolina's governor denied that their recruiting team had made any offer to purchase vehicles, and North Carolina officials stated their commitment was to buy 1,000 vehicles in one year, not the 2,000 Alabama's governor thought.[21]

To complicate further the state's commitment to purchase the 2,500 vehicles, a Birmingham lawyer filed suit in state court to block the purchase by the state or any of its entities. The lawyer argued that the commitment violated state purchasing laws and should be declared illegal and therefore nonbinding. When the case got to court, the lawyers for the state said the commitment was simply "puff" designed to lure Mercedes to Alabama. The *Birmingham News* reported: "[L]awyers for the state said in a court hearing Friday that Alabama officials never intended to buy anything without going through bid laws."[22]

The next embarrassing revelation for the governor and the state came only days later. The media revealed that the attorney for the State

Revenue Department issued an opinion that the state would be responsible for paying refunds to workers who had too much income tax withheld by their employers from their paychecks under the new industrial incentives law.[23] Since the actual percentage of tax paid by a worker depends on several factors, such as marital status and the number of dependents, the amount of refunds owed by the state to workers who have had the company withhold the 5 percent "job development fee" was unknown. The Alabama Development Office estimated earlier that the total annual benefit to Mercedes for the 5 percent withholding was approximately $42.6 million.

Of course, the new law did not apply to Mercedes exclusively but to any company that met the minimum criteria of creating fifty new jobs, investing $5 million, and paying an average wage of $8 an hour. Companies undertaking expansions in Alabama had only to create twenty new jobs and invest $2 million to take advantage of the incentives legislation.[24] These modest requirements brought "a number of companies" to apply for the tax breaks, including several that had already committed to building or expanding in Alabama. For example, Hanna Steel Corporation had earlier announced a $30 million expansion in Tuscaloosa before Mercedes had made public its choice of Alabama.[25] Hanna made its intentions known to the state that it was planning to fund its expansion utilizing the provisions of the new law.

The public relations problems continued for the governor when the Associated Press broke the following story a few days later:

> A black Mercedes-Benz with an $82,000 sticker price is waiting on Gov. Jim Folsom, Jr. at a Montgomery dealership while his staff figures out how to keep taxpayers from getting stuck with the bill.
>
> As part of the negotiations to land the Mercedes assembly plant in Tuscaloosa County, Gov. Folsom agreed to use one of the company's luxury sedans as his official state car.
>
> Mercedes officials sent a black S420 model to their Montgomery dealer.[26]

The governor's legal adviser informed the governor that he could not purchase the automobile with state funds since that action would violate the purchasing law that required competitive bids on any item over $5,000. The governor's staff reportedly sought a company or individual to lease the vehicle from Mercedes and "then re-lease it to the state for use by the governor's office, possibly for $1 per year."[27]

A state legislator requested an opinion from the State Ethics Commission on the propriety of the governor asking for corporate or individual contributions to lease the sedan for his use. He wrote: "It would seem if the governor were really concerned about the image of Alabama, he would not beg private business for money so that he could sit behind the wheel of a Mercedes-Benz."[28] The Ethics Commission executive director informed the governor's office that it was permissible for an individual or company to lease the vehicle if "the company providing the car should not do business with the state or have dealings with Mercedes-Benz and the car should not be used for political functions."[29] Several months later, the governor's press secretary announced that the governor would not use the Mercedes as his official vehicle because he already had a leased Lincoln at his disposal. She said the governor's promise to use a Mercedes as his official car was simply a "goodwill gesture" and was not binding.[30]

Another of the Alabama recruiting team's commitments to Mercedes caused a minor reaction when it was revealed that the highway from Birmingham to Tuscaloosa was to be renamed the Mercedes Highway. The location of the plant is in the small town of Vance, midway between Birmingham and Tuscaloosa. A state legislator, who was an ardent University of Alabama football fan, proposed that the highway be named after the late coach Paul Bryant and announced that he was planning to introduce a bill in the legislature to have the highway named after the coach. He asked Alabama fans across the state to contact their legislators to support his bill.

A further revelation for Alabama citizens came in a front-page article in the *Wall Street Journal* at the end of November. The newspaper reported that Alabama had committed to paying the salaries and wages of the 1,500 new employees for the first year or so. Apparently other states were not willing to accede to this request from Mercedes, as reported by the *Wall Street Journal:*

> Then came a bombshell. At a late-night meeting . . . a Mercedes official turned to ask the North Carolina Secretary of Commerce a question. Would the state pick up the salaries of its 1,500 workers for their first year or so on the job, at a cost of $45 million? The workers would be in their training then, and wouldn't be producing anything, Mercedes explained. "I was sitting next to the governor," Mr. Phillips recalls. "We were both shocked. We just said no, right out. I mean, training is one thing, but paying someone's wages?" Alabama, meanwhile, was getting similar questions, and was saying yes, yes, yes, even to the salary request.[31]

The Alabama media acknowledged that the governor and his staff had disclosed this commitment at the time of the announcement. However, it was not clearly spelled out that the state would pay the first year or so salaries and wages of the Mercedes workforce. Rather, the commitment was included under a section in the news release concerning training costs. It read that the state would pay "wages, insurance coverages (as determined by MB) allowances and per diems for employees during the training period."[32] Reporters and other observers did not realize that the training period would include at least the first year of employment for the 1,500 new workers.

What had begun as a great public relations victory for Alabama with the Mercedes announcement in Tuscaloosa in late September had turned into a public relations nightmare by the middle of November. One of the leading political columnists in the state wrote:

> In the wake of recent disclosures, I wish I had been a little less exuberant. Only now are we learning the price, the very high price, we paid to get Mercedes. The evidence mounts that Gov. Folsom and his point man, ADO Director Billy Joe Camp, promised Mercedes everything but their firstborn to locate in this state. . . . I have seen a lot of taxpayer ripoffs in my time, and this surely ranks in the Top 10. Maybe No. 1.[33]

Problems for the governor and his industrial recruitment team continued in late December when State Representative Alvin Holmes, a leader of the Legislative Black Caucus, announced that he was planning to file a bill to revoke the incentives bill used to attract Mercedes if the German auto maker did not agree to a set-aside of 30 percent of the jobs and contracts at the manufacturing facility for blacks.[34] Reportedly, he was angry because an earlier meeting with Mercedes officials was postponed when the head of the project for Mercedes broke his arm in an accident. Holmes seemed to want to antagonize Mercedes: "The German people and the German nation have a long history of racism."[35] Another state legislator added: "The German philosophy we all know from World War II forward has been a history of discrimination."[36]

The *Huntsville Times*, in response to Holmes's attack on Mercedes, editorialized:

> Actually, Germany has been acting forcefully against racist violence—more forcefully than Alabama has ever acted. . . .
>
> If these people keep it up, they may get what they want. Mercedes may get sick of the entire mess and decide to go elsewhere. And long-suffering Alabamians can again sit proudly—and defiantly—atop a social and economic pile of rubbish.[37]

In mid-January, the meeting between Mercedes officials and the black legislators took place in Montgomery. Representative Holmes was apparently satisfied after the meeting, even though the headline in the paper the next day read: "Mercedes Makes No Promises."[38] Holmes reported to the press after the closed-door meeting that Mercedes was committed to fairness: "All individuals regardless of race and color will be treated equally."[39] The Mercedes spokesman announced that the company would establish a minority advisory board with a goal of strengthening ties with minorities in the state. While Holmes did not agree to withdraw his bills to repeal the incentives law, he told the press he would not "push the bills."[40]

Shortly after the confrontation between Mercedes and the black legislators seemed to be settled, the media reported that the governor had assigned the National Guard to clear the land and prepare the construction site for Mercedes in Vance. Thirty National Guardsmen with numerous pieces of state-owned heavy equipment worked on the 1,000 acre site to shape it so that it would drain properly and allow for the building of the Mercedes plant. The Guardsmen were paid their regular active-duty wages by the state while working at the Mercedes site. The governor defended the use of the National Guard on the grounds that it was good training for the soldiers.[41]

Critics were quick to question the use of soldiers to prepare the site. One state senator claimed: "I think it's another misuse of government funds. I'm totally shocked. I think we've given Mercedes-Benz enough." Another state senator said: "I have in the past tried to get National Guardsmen to work at schools and they say they can't because they would be in competition with private business. Why can't those National Guardsmen go into some of these poor districts and build an auditorium?"[42] Trade organizations were also angry that private construction companies were not able to bid for this large job.[43]

Within days of the media criticism of the National Guard preparing the site for the Mercedes plant, the head of the Guard removed the soldiers. By the end of the month, the Tuscaloosa County Industrial Development Authority announced that it was awarding an $8 million contract to a local construction company to do the necessary site work.[44]

THE FUTURE WILL TELL

The question of whether acquiring Mercedes for Alabama was worth the price the state paid was widely debated. Advocates of the deal pointed out that Mercedes will employ 1,500 people directly and another 13,000 to 15,000 jobs may be created by spin-off industries that may be built in Alabama to supply Mercedes over the next twenty years.

Furthermore, the state projected that these new industries will invest $7.3 billion in the state over that time period. The new taxes generated by the investment should provide an enhanced quality of life for Alabama's citizens. Advocates of the Mercedes incentive package argued that the tax abatements and incentives given to the company represented money not now being received by the state, so it was not really giving away anything that it presently had.[45]

Mercedes may turn out to be the catalyst for quality economic development for Alabama and lead to the change in the image of Alabama that is so greatly sought by business leaders in the state. On the other hand, observers in Alabama appeared to assume that the new Mercedes sport utility vehicle would be successful in the market competing against Ford Explorers, Chevrolet Blazers, and Jeep Cherokees priced $10,000 to $15,000 less. If Mercedes is not successful with its new venture, it has little investment to leave in Alabama since the site and the facility are being provided to it by the state and local governments.

AN ANALYSIS

It is interesting to analyze this case study to determine what went wrong in terms of the public's perception of it. The four issues listed below that developed from the Mercedes case fall into three categories—accountability, political, and constitutional. The first two issues raise questions of accountability, the third led to a political problem, and the last a constitutional one.

1. The governor and his recruiting team made commitments beyond what the legislature had authorized in the industrial incentives law and other existing laws. Most damaging was that these commitments were not made known at the time of the public announcement but were discovered by the press only afterwards, over the following weeks. Three examples of these commitments were the promised purchase of 2,500 sport utility vehicles that would violate state purchasing laws, the agreement to lease or purchase a Mercedes sedan for use as the governor's official car, and the offer to rename the highway from Birmingham to Tuscaloosa after the auto maker.
2. The governor and his recruiters apparently were caught off guard when the attorney for the Revenue Department issued an opinion that the state would have to refund any amount withheld by the company in excess of what employees owed the state in individual income taxes.

This provision could encourage employers to withhold the maximum and let the state refund employees for their deductions based on marital status and number of dependents.

3. The governor, his ADO director, and others involved with the project alienated some existing industries in the state by their actions. The ADO director's calls for state and local agencies to purchase Mercedes vehicles to show appreciation to the auto maker for locating in the state offended the workers and management at the General Motors plant in Decatur. The governor attempted to correct this offense by visiting the plant in his Chevrolet. The erection of the Mercedes symbol at Legion Field was considered a slap in the face by large Alabama companies located in Birmingham that have employed thousands of Alabamians for decades.
4. Constitutional questions concerning the industrial incentives bill were ignored at the time of passage even though they were raised by at least one legislator. The state constitution pledges income tax revenue to support public schools and further earmarks individual income tax receipts for school teachers' salaries. The constitutional question, then, is whether the legislature has the legal authority to allow Mercedes to collect and keep income taxes paid by its workers. The consequences for the Mercedes commitment are significant. If the court declares unconstitutional the industrial incentives law, one of two things could happen: Mercedes could withdraw its commitment to build in Alabama or the governor and the legislature could submit the question of amending the constitution to the citizens. If the referendum on the amendment fails, then it would be unlikely that Mercedes would build its plant in Alabama.

CONCLUSION

This case study of the efforts of various southern states to attract the Mercedes plant illustrates dramatically how the competition for industrial development has brought the issue of incentives to the attention of the American public through the media. The call by the National Governors' Association and other organizations to bring the incentives competition under control has not been heeded. For there to be meaningful restraint on the incentives war, the states will have to agree on certain limits among themselves. It is unlikely that the federal government will feel that it has an interest in intervening as long as federal revenues or other national interests are not affected. The public and media reaction to the

Mercedes deal both inside and outside Alabama may prove to be the factor that leads to meaningful reform by states on their own or in conjunction with each other.

NOTES

1. Associated Press, "Mercedes-Benz Plans to Build Utility Vehicle Plant in U.S.," *Columbus Ledger-Enquirer*, 6 April 1993, B11.
2. John D. Milazzo, "Mercedes Driving for Decision by October," *Montgomery Advertiser*, 4 September 1993, 10A.
3. Associated Press, "Rumors: Mercedes Steering for Alabama," *Montgomery Advertiser*, 29 September 1993, 9A.
4. Jim Wooten, "New Rules in Game of Giveaways," *Atlanta Journal*, 28 November 1993, F5.
5. Associated Press, "Mercedes Reportedly Considering Site Near Charleston," *Montgomery Advertiser*, 8 August 1993, 7B.
6. Associated Press, "State Aims to Lure Mercedes Plant," *Columbus Ledger-Enquirer*, 6 August 1993, A3.
7. Associated Press, "Rumors: Mercedes Steering for Alabama," 9A.
8. Associated Press, "Council OKs Mercedes Site Funding," *Montgomery Advertiser*, 22 September 1993, 5B.
9. Associated Press, "State Aims to Lure Mercedes Plant," A3.
10. Helene Cooper and Glenn Ruffenach, "Mercedes Expected to Choose Alabama for Plant, But State's Price Will Be Steep," *Wall Street Journal*, 30 September 1993, A2 and A12.
11. David Rountree, "Benz Cites Quality for Choice," *Montgomery Advertiser*, 1 October 1993, 1A.
12. Jay Reeves, "Alabama Basks in Official Unveiling of Mercedes-Benz Deal," *Columbus Ledger-Enquirer*, 1 October 1993, A1.
13. James E. Jacobson, ed., "Camp's Cars," *Birmingham News*, 25 October 1993, 4A.
14. Jeffrey Hansen, "They'll Look Twice at Alabama," *Birmingham News*, 10 October 1993, 1D.
15. Cooper and Ruffenach, "Mercedes Expected to Choose Alabama for Plant, But State's Price Will Be Steep," A2.
16. Hansen, "They'll Look Twice at Alabama," 1D.
17. Wooten, "New Rules in Game of Giveaways," F5.
18. Jacobsen, "Camp's Cars," 4A.
19. Ibid.
20. David Pace, "State's Offer Saved Deal, Folsom Says," *Montgomery Advertiser*, 9 November 1993, 3B.

21. Ibid.

22. Robin DeMonia, "Governor Backs Off Use of Mercedes as Official Car," *Birmingham News*, 19 March 1994, 10A.

23. Jay Reeves, "Tax Law Worth Millions to Mercedes," *Montgomery Advertiser*, 12 November 1993, 1A.

24. Associated Press, "New Guidelines Set for Tax Incentives," *Montgomery Advertiser*, 21 January 1994, 5B.

25. Associated Press, "Other Companies Are Already Trying to Use Mercedes Bill," *Opelika-Auburn News*, 12 November 1993, A2.

26. Associated Press, "$82,000 Mercedes Ready for Folsom," *Montgomery Advertiser*, 20 November 1993, 1A.

27. John D. Milazzo, "Mercedes Deal Hits Another Bump," *Montgomery Advertiser*, 23 November 1993, 1A and 4A.

28. Ibid.

29. Staff, "Ethics Chief Warns Folsom of Using Cars," *Montgomery Advertiser*, 24 November 1993, 3B.

30. DeMonia, "Governor Backs Off Use of Mercedes as Official Car," 1A.

31. E. S. Browning and Helene Cooper, "States' Bidding War over Mercedes Plant Made for Costly Chase," *Wall Street Journal*, 24 November 1993, A6. See also Kenneth Hare, ed., "'Free' Enterprise," *Montgomery Advertiser*, 29 November 1993, 10A.

32. Ibid.

33. Bob Ingram, "Mercedes Praise Turns to Ashes," *Montgomery Advertiser*, 14 November 1993, 1F.

34. Stephen Merelman, "Bills Target Mercedes Benefits," *Montgomery Advertiser*, 28 December 1993, 3B.

35. Ibid.

36. Ibid.

37. Reprinted on editorial page, *Montgomery Advertiser*, 1 January 1994, 12A.

38. Stephen Merelman, "Mercedes Makes No Promises," *Montgomery Advertiser*, 19 January 1994, 3B.

39. Ibid.

40. Ibid.

41. David Rynecki, "Folsom Calls on Guard for Benz Site," *Birmingham Post-Herald*, 21 January 1994, A1 and A3.

42. Ibid.

43. Ibid.

44. Associated Press, "Northport Company Gets $8 Million Mercedes Job," *Montgomery Advertiser*, 31 January 1994, 2B.

45. Craig Woodward, "State to Reap Benefits of Mercedes Incentives," *Montgomery Advertiser*, 31 October 1993, 1F.

6 Federal Government Affects Local Competition

In addition to the assistance local governments receive from their state governments in economic development, they are also able to tap a number of resources available from the federal government to aid them in their competition with other localities for economic growth. Local governments depend on assistance from the federal government to strengthen their positions economically through various means. In this chapter, many of the key roles played by the federal government in local economic development will be explored. No attempt will be made to examine those programs or projects that aid citizens or businesses directly unless they are channeled through local governments.

The federal government affects every citizen and business in the United States directly and profoundly. Obviously, any attempt to detail all of the ways the federal government influences local economies would consume volumes. It is our purpose here to examine some of the major ways in which the federal government affects local economies and makes them more viable as economic entities. While some of these programs are available to all localities, many of them are redistributive—that is, they take resources from one area and move them to another area determined by federal policymakers to be in greater need. The programs that are redistributive are intended to give an advantage to recipient governments in their competition with other local governments.

Local economic development agencies look to the federal government to assist them through grants and through tax policy. In the first section, we will review the federal role in awarding or granting funds to local governments for economic development. In the next section, the implications of federal tax policy on local economic development will be explored.

GRANT ASSISTANCE FOR LOCAL ECONOMIC DEVELOPMENT

As has been documented extensively elsewhere, the federal government's role in assisting local governments through grants sharply declined in the 1980s.[1] Most of the direct aid from the federal government in the 1950s, 1960s, and 1970s was in the form of improving infrastructure or providing housing opportunities for low- and moderate-income citizens. Federal aid to cities reached its high point in the years of the Johnson and Nixon administrations. Johnson's Great Society produced hundreds of new federal aid programs within a span of several years. For example, there were 379 new grant programs approved by Congress in 1966 at the height of the Great Society.[2] Nixon's New Federalism created general revenue sharing for the states and localities and led to the passage of the Community Development Block Grant (CDBG) program during the Ford administration in 1974. CDBG remains the primary federal aid program for cities.

During the Carter administration, a new approach to federal aid for local economic development was implemented. Carter recommended to Congress that the federal government assist needy cities and counties by providing funds that could be used to entice private investors to build facilities and create jobs. For eleven years (1978–1989), Congress designated the UDAG program to assist distressed cities and urban counties in their economic development efforts. The 1977 legislation authorizing UDAG directed HUD to use the funds in "severely distressed cities and urban counties to help alleviate physical and economic deterioration."[3]

UDAG differed from other federal programs in its emphasis on public-private partnerships. Most other federal programs assisted local governments with building infrastructure—such as water tanks, sewage treatment plants, or streets—with the expectation that economic development would happen as a result of the infrastructure improvements. For example, the urban renewal program of the 1960s and early 1970s funded the construction of such infrastructure as industrial parks and water tanks without direct commitments from companies that they would locate in the communities for which Urban Renewal built the new facilities.

Under UDAG, however, local governments were required to negotiate with the private sector for financial commitments to projects that investors were planning to build before applying for UDAG assistance. The UDAG supplemental assistance was to be used to bridge financial gaps in projects or provide necessary infrastructure that prevented private sector investment from otherwise proceeding. UDAGs were intended solely for development projects that were privately sponsored, financed, and managed. Examples of projects for which UDAGs were approved by HUD included new industrial plants, hotels, and office buildings. The projects had to create jobs for low- and moderate-income citizens and strengthen the local government's tax base. Applications from cities or counties to build infrastructure in the hopes of creating development or jobs were not accepted.

Over the life of the UDAG program, Congress appropriated $4.6 billion for projects that fell in one of three categories—industrial, commercial, or housing (neighborhood). One-fourth of the funds were set aside for small cities, which competed for funds separately from large cities. (The case studies of two small cities in Alabama, Auburn and Bessemer, that were very successful in the UDAG competition were presented in chapter 3). At the end of the program, HUD claimed that nearly $32 billion of private funds and over $1.9 billion in other public funds had been invested in its UDAG projects. Commercial projects received half of the UDAG funds; industrial projects, 24 percent; housing projects, 11 percent; and mixed projects, 15 percent. Nearly two-thirds of the funds granted to local governments were used as loans to developers. As a result, local governments should receive nearly $1 billion in loan paybacks by the mid-1990s.[4] HUD encouraged cities to create revolving loan funds with the paybacks, so that the money received by the local governments could be used to generate additional economic development. Examples of cities using UDAG paybacks to create RLFs are found in chapters 2 and 3.

The UDAG program was recommended by the Carter administration as a supplement to the CDBG program, which initially did not allow communities to use grant funds for economic development.[5] During the Reagan administration, Congress amended the law so that CDBG could be used for economic development projects as well as other community improvement efforts. In recent years, entitlement cities have devoted a sizable portion of their CDBG allotments to economic development. According to HUD's 1989 report to Congress on CDBG, approximately one-fifth of total CDBG allocations to entitlement cities are spent on economic development. Likewise, states have used an average of nearly 22 percent of their CDBG funds for economic development since economic development became an eligible activity in the early 1980s.[6]

One method that states use in ensuring that their CDBG funds are used in the areas or for the purposes they desire is special set-asides. Set-asides are funds earmarked for particular purposes or for certain geographic areas within the states. The largest set-aside by far is for economic development, with thirty-eight states earmarking funds for the purpose of creating jobs or stimulating investment.[7]

HUD, in its report to Congress, pointed out the types of economic development projects funded by CDBG:

> Loans and grants to businesses for the rehabilitation, expansion and construction of commercial and industrial buildings and facilities, and the purchase of equipment. . . . Infrastructure improvements, such as industrial park development, parking additions, streets and sidewalks, and other improvements designed to make sites more attractive places to do business. . . .
>
> Other activities include facade improvements and commercial revitalization, land acquisition, clearing structures, packaging land for industrial parks, and encouraging commercial and industrial redevelopment; and technical, small and minority business, and economic development assistance.[8]

Primarily through CDBG, the federal government still plays an important role in the economic development activities of local governments despite the reduction in the number of grant programs since the late 1960s and the 1970s. This is especially true in the nation's larger cities that receive CDBG funds automatically as entitlement communities under the Housing and Community Development Act of 1974. These cities have devoted a sizable percentage of the funds they receive annually for economic development activities. In addition to CDBG, some cities continue to benefit from repaid UDAG dollars generated between 1978 and 1989.

In addition to the HUD programs, other grant programs of the federal government are available to the nation's localities. Some of the grant programs send funds directly to local governments, such as those administered by the Economic Development Administration, while others indirectly affect local governments. Examples of the latter are programs that aid the elderly through a national network of aging agencies, children through various welfare programs and Head Start, the sick through Medicare and Medicaid, small businesses through the Small Business Administration, and students through student loans as well as direct aid to schools and colleges. All of these programs pump money into local economies as well as address social problems of communities.

TAX POLICY INFLUENCES LOCAL DEVELOPMENT

Congress also influences local economic development through tax policy. Prior to 1986, there was little restraint on the ability of local agencies to issue tax-free bonds for private companies. State and local issuance of tax-exempt bonds increased significantly from 1965, when total bond sales equaled $11.1 billion.[9] By 1985, bond sales peaked at $204.3 billion, which represented a remarkable 14.6 percent annual increase.[10]

Congress became concerned over this rapid increase for two reasons. First, federal officials estimated the revenue lost to the U.S. Treasury by 1985 at $18.5 billion per year and predicted that the total would continue to rise rapidly each year. Second, concern was expressed that the bonds were increasingly being used for purposes not consistent with the original intent of the law. As mentioned previously, local industrial development boards had issued bonds for many questionable projects, such as the construction of large numbers of Kmart stores and McDonald's restaurants. This obvious movement away from the original intent of industrial development bonds by local governments contributed to the severe restrictions imposed by Congress in the 1986 Tax Reform Act.

In testimony before the Senate Committee on Small Business in 1985, Assistant Treasury Secretary Ronald A. Pearlman stated:

> I think it is generally acknowledged, that tax exempt financing is simply an indirect subsidy by the Federal Government and maybe by the State government also if it provides tax exemption to private business. The industrial development bond, the small issue IDB, . . . is a good example of that. It simply makes available low cost funds to business.[11]

Pearlman further argued that the federal government would not provide an across-the-board subsidy if the question were considered during the appropriation process.[12] Users of tax-free bonds made a budgetary choice for the Congress, in effect, without any direct consideration by Congress —not as an appropriation but through the giving away of revenue that otherwise would go to the U.S. Treasury.

Since the intent of Congress, which was to encourage industrial growth by granting industrial development bonds tax-free status, was violated, new restrictions were placed on all private-activity bonds in the Tax Reform Act of 1986. In effect, tax-free bonds could no longer be used as a weapon by local agencies in their efforts to create commercial development in their communities. Their use in industrial development was also severely curtailed.[13] However, Congress has extended the limited right of local governments to use tax-free IDBs several times since the passage of the 1986 Act. Apparently, there has been congressional support for the use of tax-free bonds to encourage manufacturing expansion.

The 1986 Tax Reform Act produced major changes in the tax-exempt municipal bond market. The Public Securities Association calculated that approximately 41 percent of all bonds issued in 1984 could not have been issued in 1991 as tax exempt under the 1986 law.[14] The net effect of the changes made by Congress to the tax law in 1986 was that local economic development agencies were greatly restricted in their uses of federal tax policy as a weapon in economic development.

COMPETITION FOR FEDERAL FACILITIES

The federal government is generally thought of in terms of its governmental role in distributing its resources to people or places to achieve some national objective. However, from the perspective of local governments, the federal government is viewed in a second, and very different, way. The federal government is much like an industry in that it has facilities and jobs that bolster local economies. For that reason, local governments compete for the location of federal facilities just as they do for a new industrial plant or any other major development. In this market role, the federal government is a buyer and the localities are sellers. Ideally, the local area must have an attractive and adequate location, trained workforce, and good transportation network, among other things, to "sell" to the federal government before a facility is located there.

While the major projects and facilities of the federal government are sought after by numerous local governments just as vigorously as are manufacturing facilities, an interesting added dimension to this competition is the political one. Normally, the competing local governments enlist their senators or representatives to fight for their causes to bring federal projects or facilities to their areas. The success of Senator Robert Byrd in bringing federal installations to West Virginia was widely noted in the media in the early 1990s.[15] Byrd was instrumental in locating a new NASA facility in Fairmont, a new FBI building in Clarksburg, and Coast Guard and IRS installations in Martinsburg. In an earlier era, Representative Mendel Rivers of South Carolina, as chairman of the House Armed Services Committee, was well known for bringing military installations to his district in Charleston.

In the post–cold war era, the practice of earmarking federal funds, especially from the Defense Department budget, by members of Congress for pet projects back home has become even more commonplace. In 1991, $1.4 billion was earmarked for nonmilitary spending from the defense budget; in 1993, the amount had increased to $4.6 billion, or 2 percent of the total defense budget.[16] Projects in the budget included such things as museums, sports jamborees, medical research, antidrug efforts, and the Claude Pepper Memorial Foundation.

Mark Thompson reported:

> Rep. John Murtha, D-Pa., chairman of the House Appropriations defense subcommittee, has siphoned hundreds of millions of federal dollars to his district. In the 1994 Pentagon budget, for example, he got $70 million earmarked for his alma mater, the University of Pittsburgh. . . .
>
> Murtha also directed the Pentagon to spend $50 million to build a National Drug Intelligence Center in Johnstown, which is his hometown. The center ended up there "because that's where I wanted it," he told reporters at its dedication in August.[17]

While the practice of earmarking federal funds by influential legislators is not fair to other localities, it is generally believed by local officials that the location of a major federal facility in a community has a substantial impact on the local economy and is worth pursuing through the political process if necessary. As a result, local governments compete strongly for these facilities, some through political methods and some through legitimate competition. An example is the fierce competition for the multibillion-dollar supercollider project that eventually was located in Texas but subsequently was terminated. Another example is the competition by the numerous port cities along the Gulf Coast during the 1980s to be the new homeport for the U.S. Navy (which will be explored in more detail in the case study in the next chapter).

A third example is the competition for space funds spent through NASA. These installations are especially sought after because they bring highly educated and well-paid scientists to a community. When the House of Representatives approved further funding for NASA's space station, the Associated Press reported the reaction in Huntsville, Alabama, where much of the space station work is being conducted:

> Huntsville officials, encouraged by House approval of the space station, said jobs and economic development remain at stake with a Senate vote ahead.
>
> Huntsville Mayor Steve Hettinger said the demise of the project would be unsettling for the area.
>
> "It would have been bad news from the standpoint of jobs and our economic development," Mayor Hettinger said.[18]

In the post–cold war era, the presence of major Defense Department facilities in a community has a serious downside. As the military is restructured to conform to the new realities of the post–cold war era, many military facilities are being closed or sharply reduced through the Defense Base Closure and Realignment Commission. There are at least three major impacts on a local economy as a result of the closure of a military facility. The first is that military personnel assigned to the facility move from the community and no longer spend their money in local businesses; second, local suppliers no longer have a substantial market for their goods; and third, the local civilians who work at the federal facility no longer have jobs there.

Cities that have traditionally enjoyed a stable economy because of the presence of military facilities are now faced with the prospect, or reality, of high unemployment caused directly by the loss of jobs at the facility and in the support businesses in the community that depend on the facility for their livelihoods. In the face of losing a substantial part of their economic bases, local governments and community business leaders have realized that they must become competitive with other communities for private sector growth if they are to survive. The reaction by leaders in Pensacola, Florida, to the news that the Navy was to close its facilities in that city was typical of the response of most communities. Leaders, both political and business, called for the development of a strategy to diversify the local economy. Many of the strategies used by competitive cities were discussed by community leaders as now being necessary for Pensacola.

The Department of Defense issued a report in 1993 on the status of the civilian reuse of closed military bases from 1961 to 1993. The department's conclusion was that localities had fared well after the military has left:

- On the basis of a survey of 97 closed bases, 171,177 new jobs have more than replaced the loss of 87,557 DoD civilian jobs at the former bases.
- Four year colleges and post-secondary vocational technical schools or community colleges have been established at 36 former bases with an estimated annual enrollment of 124,045 students.
- In addition to the college enrollments, education uses have also been established at 21 former bases with 20,344 high school vo-tech students and 37,593 vocational trainees.
- Industrial and office parks are located at more than 83 former bases.
- Municipal and general aviation airports are located at 43 former DoD facilities.
- Civilian reuse at the former military bases has been achieved by the local communities. Local community leaders are the real heroes in this adjustment process. . . .
- Complete base redevelopment requires a long-term commitment, sometimes up to 20 years for some bases.

- Communities can recover effectively from base closures. Adjustments can provide long-term opportunities—not necessarily a crisis.[19]

We know that senators and representatives almost always play a key role in the location of federal facilities. Oftentimes, the decision to place a facility in one location rather than another is based solely on political considerations. It can sometimes work the other way as well. When Senator Richard Shelby of Alabama challenged President Clinton's economic reform package, the president threatened to move ninety jobs associated with the space program from the Marshall Space Flight Center in Huntsville, Alabama, to the Johnson Space Center in Houston, Texas. The senator toned down his public criticism of the president after the president visited Shelby at his home in Washington. Months later, a NASA spokesman announced that the jobs would not be moved from Huntsville because the move might "increase the possibility of error" on space shuttle launches.[20]

CONCLUSION

The federal government serves as a provider of weapons in the economic development war for local governments through grants-in-aid, as an influence on the incentives states and localities have the ability to grant to businesses through tax policy, and as a source of economic development prizes in the form of federal installations to be won by local governments. Recent history has shown that all can be less than reliable. Federal grants to local governments to aid in economic development have been sharply curtailed. Many of the tax incentives used by local governments, especially in the South, were either eliminated or limited by Congress in the Tax Reform Act of 1986. And the closing of military installations, the elimination of programs such as the supercollider, and the threat to discontinue programs such as the space station and the Navy's homeport demonstrates the tenuous nature of federal facilities for communities.

The next chapter will present a case study of the efforts of Mobile, Alabama, and other Gulf Coast cities to secure a new Navy homeport in the mid-1980s. The Navy announced that it was planning to establish a new homeport for its fleet and requested port cities along the Gulf of Mexico to submit proposals if they wished to be considered for this economic development prize. The city selected as the homeport expected hundreds of new jobs and millions of federal dollars for the local economy. The competition among the Gulf of Mexico port cities to serve as the Navy's homeport was fierce. The Navy's decision resulted in nine sites selected rather than one. Mobile was one of the winners, but the prize did not turn out to be what local leaders had hoped it would be.

NOTES

1. Lillian Rymarowicz and Dennis Zimmerman, "Federal Budget and Tax Policy and the State-Local Sector: Retrenchment in the 1980s," *CRS Report for Congress* (Washington, D.C.: Library of Congress, 9 September 1988), 2.

2. Ibid. See also Douglas J. Watson and Thomas Vocino, "The Changing Nature of Intergovernmental Fiscal Relationships: Impact of the 1986 Tax Reform Act on State and Local Governments," *Public Administration Review* 50, no. 4 (1991), 428.

3. Douglas J. Watson, "Importance of Local Initiative in Targeting of Federal Aid: The Case of UDAGs," *Public Budgeting and Financial Management* (forthcoming).

4. Ibid.

5. Douglas J. Watson, John G. Heilman, and Robert S. Montjoy, *The Politics of Redistributing Urban Aid* (Westport, Conn.: Praeger Publishers, 1994), 45.

6. U.S. Department of Housing and Urban Development, Office of Community Planning and Development, *Report to Congress on Community Development Programs—1989* (Washington, D.C.: U.S. Department of Housing and Urban Development, 1989), 28.

7. Ibid., 29.

8. Ibid., 15–16.

9. The following three paragraphs may be found in Watson and Vocino, 428–33.

10. Rymarowicz and Zimmerman, 18.

11. U.S. Congress, Senate Committee on Small Business, *Small Issue Industrial Development Bonds: Hearings before the Subcommittee on Small Business: Family Farm*, 99th Cong., 1st Sess., 11 June 1985, 262.

12. Ibid.

13. Dennis Zimmerman, "Tax Reform: Its Potential Effect on the State and Local Sector," *CRS Report for Congress* (Washington, D.C.: Library of Congress, 20 March 1987).

14. Lee Ann Pierce, "Tax Exempt Bonds," *South Dakota Law Review* 32, no. 3 (1987), 525.

15. Mark Thompson, "Congress Forcing Pet Projects into Pentagon's Budget," *Columbus (Georgia) Ledger-Enquirer*, 15 December 1993, A1 and A4.

16. Ibid.

17. Ibid.

18. Associated Press, "Huntsville Officials Praise Space Station Vote by House," *Montgomery (Alabama) Advertiser*, 30 June 1993, 5D.

19. U.S. Department of Defense, Office of Economic Adjustment, *Civilian Reuse of Former Military Bases* (Washington, D.C.: U.S. Department of Defense, 1993), 4.

20. Associated Press, "Project for Shuttle to Stay at Marshall," *Montgomery Advertiser*, 24 December 1993, 2B.

7 Gulf Coast Homeports Come (and Go)

The federal government has numerous facilities that employ thousands of people and serve as anchors for many local economies. So when the federal government announces that it is planning to build or relocate a facility, such as a military base, local leaders are anxious to compete for it. This chapter examines the efforts of Mobile, Alabama, and other Gulf Coast communities to become homeports for the U.S. Navy during the mid-1980s. The case study will demonstrate that the Navy behaved much like an industry does in encouraging local and state governments to commit resources to the project in the form of incentives. Sixteen localities along the Gulf Coast responded to the competition by developing proposals for the Navy with millions of dollars of state and local money committed to the project if the Navy selected their sites.

The added dimension in competition for federal facilities is the political one. In this case study, elected officials on all levels became very active players in an effort to entice the Navy to choose their communities. It is likely that political considerations altered the outcome from what would have happened if it were a private company selecting a site. Instead of designating one homeport on the Gulf of Mexico among the six finalists, the secretary of the Navy named nine cities to share in the project. Three of the cities were not even listed among the six finalists but were awarded some of the ships designated for the new homeport. The result was that members of Congress and governors from Texas, Mississippi, Louisiana, Florida, and Alabama were able to claim successes as a result of their efforts. Most, especially Republicans, were quick to capitalize politically on the Reagan administration's announcement of the new homeports, as will be shown in the case study.

WHAT IS STRATEGIC HOMEPORTING?

From 1964 to 1973, the number of active ships in the U.S. Navy was reduced from 917 to 523. As a result, the Navy had twice as many homeports as it needed and decided to consolidate its facilities in 1973.[1] The Navy believed that it needed two homeports on each coast for each class of ships. Carriers, for example, were homeported in Norfolk, Virginia, and Mayport, Florida, on the East Coast and in San Diego and Alameda, California, on the West Coast.[2] While there were some critics of the plan to eliminate some of the homeports in 1973, the reduced number of homeports seemed to satisfy the needs of the downsized Navy.

However, following the election of President Ronald Reagan and his subsequent appointment of John Lehman as secretary of the Navy, an enlarged role for the Navy in the country's defense plans became a priority. The Reagan administration, through Lehman, proposed a goal to increase the Navy to 600 ships and found support in Congress to fund the construction of the new vessels. With the 170 or more new ships slated for the Navy, the number of homeports and the facilities available at each now were inadequate. In congressional testimony in 1985 on the 600-ship Navy, Secretary Lehman argued that it would be unwise to locate any more ships in the existing homeports because they were already "dangerously packed."[3] The choice was to spend large sums either upgrading the existing homeports or building new homeports.

Lehman argued that new homeports were necessary for strategic reasons. In its 1982 strategic homeporting plan, the Navy, according to the General Accounting Office (GAO), stated "that the dispersal of ships to more ports and to less concentrated ports would improve U.S. defensive posture, complicate conventional warfare targeting by a potential enemy, and minimize the risks associated with a relatively simple but properly placed attack."[4]

Lehman's plan called for new homeports in the Northeast United States for a battleship surface-action group, one in the Northwest for a carrier battlegroup, one along the Gulf Coast for a battleship surface-action group and a carrier battlegroup, and one on the West Coast for a battleship surface-action group. The new homeports would serve as bases for thirty-six ships for the two carrier groups and the two battleship groups, as well as for twenty-three ships used for the Naval Reserve Force and five miscellaneous support ships.[5]

Since the new homeports were seen as threats to the continued prosperity of the existing homeports, there was considerable opposition to the plan by both Navy top brass and Congress. Lehman explained after he left the Navy the problems he faced in gaining the support of Navy leadership for the homeport concept:

> "It simply does not make sense to have the kind of concentration of the fleet in Norfolk and San Diego that we have today. You don't see Army bases with six divisions all clumped together. You don't see Air Force bases with six air wings on one base."
>
> But he admitted that he had to drag the Navy leadership, kicking and screaming, into the fold.
>
> "If the brass had their way," Lehman said, "there'd be only one homeport on the West Coast, San Diego, and one on the East Coast. That would be Hampton Roads.
>
> "The brass would like to stay in San Diego and Tidewater and in Florida and Charleston," Lehman said, "because that's where all their friends are. There are some 400 retired admirals in the San Diego community. That's where all the golf clubs are, the military hospitals, the warm weather."[6]

Members of Congress representing districts that already had major Navy facilities were not supportive of building new homeports that might negatively impact their districts. For example, Representative Owen B. Pickett of Virginia was elected to Congress primarily on his promise to do all that he could to defeat the homeporting concept. He argued that spreading the fleet gave the Navy little strategic advantage because the enemy could easily add a few more targets when it "was sitting there with 10,000 warheads."[7]

A strong ally of those in Congress who opposed the homeporting concept was the GAO, the congressional watchdog agency. In January 1985, Senator Strom Thurmond of South Carolina, who chaired the Subcommittee on Military Construction of the Committee on Armed Services, requested the GAO "to compare the cost of expanding existing homeports to handle additional ships with the cost to open new homeports."[8] The GAO concluded that the homeport idea was a bad one on every count and charged the Navy with underestimating the cost of building and operating the new homeports. While agreeing that building new homeports would be more expensive than expanding current ones, Navy officials had stated that the cost differences were "relatively small" compared to the total Navy budget over a five-year period. The GAO told Congress that the Navy's $799 million estimate did not include numerous items that would require further funding from Congress.[9]

The 1985 GAO report to Congress included this advice:

> GAO believes the Congress needs to be aware of the total budgetary impact of the Navy's strategic homeporting plan. This is particularly

> important given the prospect for defense budgets with real little growth and the over $1.8 billion in military construction deficiencies at existing homeports that will have to compete for funds with the Navy's strategic homeporting plan. There will also be additional recurring costs that the Navy has determined will be required to operate and maintain the new homeports as well as existing homeports.[10]

Despite the GAO's warnings, the political opposition within Congress, and the reluctance of Navy leadership to endorse the homeporting concept, Congress continued to approve funds for it. However, apparently in response to the GAO study, Congress enacted Public Law 99-591 in 1986 that "required that no more than $799 million would be appropriated or obligated through fiscal year 1991 for military construction for the strategic homeporting concept."[11]

By 1984, the Navy had already selected sites for new homeports for three of the regions it was targeting: Staten Island, New York, on the East Coast; Everett, Washington, in the Northwest; and San Francisco (Treasure Island) on the West Coast. Only the choice of the site along the Gulf of Mexico remained to be selected.

MOBILE AND ITS GULF COAST COMPETITORS

The first information that Mobile, Alabama, community leaders heard about the possibility of the Navy building a homeport on the Gulf Coast came in a news release from their senator Howell Heflin. Senator Heflin told the mayor and other leaders that he had heard of the Navy's plans while "snooping around" the Pentagon, and suggested that Mobile organize if it was interested in competing for the facility.[12] A thirteen-member steering committee was established that included the three members of the City Commission, three county commissioners, the director of the Alabama State Docks, several leading businessmen, and staff members from the Chamber of Commerce. The chairman of the steering committee was Robert M. Hope, also the director of the State Docks. The State Docks, a state agency, served as the representative of the governor in the recruitment process. The staff executive for the steering committee was David Toenes, the vice president of the Chamber of Commerce who worked with the military on projects for Mobile for twenty-eight years. Toenes played a key role in Mobile's homeport program for eight years.

During the next year (1984), members of the steering committee made regular visits to Washington to meet with Navy officials who were working on the homeporting program. Since no official announcement had been made about the Navy seeking proposals from communities for the Gulf Coast homeport, members of the task force simply promoted Mobile as a good site for any future Navy facility. In addition, the steering committee stayed in constant communication with members of Alabama's congressional delegation, especially Representative Herbert L. (Sonny) Callahan, a Republican who represented Mobile; and Senator Jeremiah Denton, a Republican from Mobile and a retired admiral who was a national hero for his demonstrated devotion to his country while a POW in Vietnam.

In September 1984, the Navy issued a request for proposals (RFP) from communities that were interested in serving as the homeport on the Gulf Coast. The RFP was similar to those that economic developers receive regularly from companies interested in finding locations for their factories. Communities were expected to include specific sites, a financial plan for constructing the facility, commitments from the state and local governments, industrial support capabilities, and quality-of-life considerations. Sixteen communities on the Gulf Coast responded to the RFP within the next few months. By early 1985, the Navy eliminated ten of the communities and named Mobile, Pascagoula (Mississippi), Houston/Galveston, Corpus Christi, Lake Charles (Louisiana), and Pensacola as the six finalists.

During the early months of 1985, the Navy reviewed the proposals from the six finalists, visited the sites, and met with community and political leaders. In early April 1985, the *Mobile Press Register* reported:

> The eight-member Navy study team looking over Mobile's potential as a battleship surface action group homeport donned tennis shoes Thursday afternoon to tour Pinto Island, the proposed Navy site.
>
> The study team . . . walked around the island for more than an hour, checking boundary lines and checking the condition of the property.
>
> Capt. James Ridge, the head of the site selection team, said by the end of the group's visit on Friday "we'll have a firm understanding of exactly what Mobile is proposing, and you'll know exactly what the Navy is looking for."[13]

The Navy study team visited all six cities, as the media reported in each city during the visits.

The Navy purposely sought contributions from the communities to demonstrate to Congress that there was widespread support for the homeporting concept. In addition, as Hartmann points out, the Navy tried to keep the cost down so that Congress "would not balk at the expense of adding infrastructure to a number of new bases."[14] Since

Congress had placed an upper limit of $799 million on what it would appropriate for the new homeports, the Navy was anxious to have the communities pay for as much of the infrastructure costs as they were willing to do.

Each of the finalists responded to the Navy's call for them to share in the cost of developing the homeport by offering generous incentives to the Navy to build the homeport in their communities. For example, Governor George Wallace of Alabama told the Navy study team, when its members visited him, that Alabama would spend "whatever money is necessary to make the facility acceptable to the Navy."[15] Wallace pledged to use for this project at least $40 million in cash that was available from an earlier bond issue for improvements to the State Docks. Wallace also committed the state to the construction of access roads to the proposed site for the Navy base and planned to use State Highway Department funds to pay for them.

In addition, the Mobile proposal included a pledge from the local governments, specifically the city of Mobile, that it would purchase the privately owned land that it had proposed to the Navy for the homeport and give it to the Navy. The land had been appraised at approximately $11 million, and the City Commission planned to issue bonds to pay for it. Other incentives from Mobile included the construction of a Naval Activities Center for use by Navy personnel and their families. Representative Callahan promised to raise private funds to build the center if the Navy selected Mobile.[16]

Pascagoula's proposal to the Navy included leasing ninety state-owned acres to the Navy "at minimal cost." In addition, the state and local governments pledged to build a $17 million causeway linking the island on which the base would be located to the mainland. The state of Mississippi also suggested that it would underwrite the bonds for the construction of the homeport, if the Navy wanted to use bond financing for the construction. The Pascagoula proposal also included the construction of a community center for the sailors and their dependents. In addition, the local utilities agreed to waive all utility deposits for Navy personnel once they moved to Pascagoula. Another interesting twist to the Pascagoula proposal was a commitment from local doctors and businesses that they would give discounts to all Navy personnel assigned to the homeport.[17]

Galveston and Houston filed a joint proposal to the Navy and pledged to give the Navy 125 acres south of Galveston, approximately eight miles from the Gulf of Mexico.[18] The state of Texas also offered to contribute $25 million to the project. Corpus Christi offered the Navy two sites, each of which consisted of more than 200 acres. The state's offer of $25 million also applied to the Corpus Christi site if it was selected. Corpus Christi local officials held a bond referendum in which they secured approval from the voters to donate another $25 million in local funds to the project.[19]

Possibly the best financial offer came from Lake Charles, which offered the Navy 217 acres twenty-two miles from the Gulf. Willis Noland, president of the Lake Charles Harbor and Terminal Authority, committed to do whatever dredging the Navy needed along the channel:

> Noland said the cost to the Navy will be nearly nonexistent if Louisiana were selected for the port.
>
> "I'd say if money can get it, we'll buy it," Noland said, citing a promise from Gov. Edwin Edwards to spend whatever it costs to bring the Navy there. Louisiana legislators have promised $50 million for the site, and local officials have promised to find money for the necessary dredging.[20]

Pensacola's offer included donation of acreage from the Naval Air Station located there, which would eliminate the cost of land for the Navy. Florida legislators considered offering 75 percent of the estimated $35 million total cost, and the county commission passed a one-cent sales tax for one year to raise the difference.[21]

All six communities wanted to attract the Navy's new facility because of the economic advantage that they believed a new homeport would give them. The commitments they made were based on the understanding that only one community would be selected and that it would receive the full benefit of the homeport. Mobile estimated that the homeport would bring 3,500 Navy personnel and 4,000 dependents to Mobile with an annual payroll of $60 million. The initial construction of the facility, estimated to be $100 million, would create hundreds of jobs for local companies and workers.

Secretary Lehman had promised the communities that a decision would be made in late spring or early summer once all the site visits were concluded. The political pressure on Lehman was constant from members of Congress from the Gulf Coast states under consideration. For example, then-Representative Trent Lott, who represented Pascagoula, contacted the Navy "at least once a day. We just want to make sure they remember Pascagoula."[22]

The *Houston Post* reported:

> The pressure is definitely ON. They call him almost every day now—powerful people, all wanting the same thing. He knows he can't satisfy them all. If he doesn't play his cards exactly right, their anger and vengefulness could dog him the rest of his career.

> John Lehman, the man in the middle, has his own peculiar ways of handling the stress. "I enjoy it," the secretary of Navy confesses. He smiles a little at his own perversity. . . .
>
> Though he has been subject to some powerful persuasions from "strong armtwisters" in the five state congressional delegations that are vying for the *Wisconsin*, the Navy secretary insists that politics "will not determine which of the ports gets chosen. That I can state categorically."[23]

Lehman, several days after this interview, made his announcement of the Navy's choice for the Gulf Coast homeport. Apparently, Lehman did his best to satisfy all the powerful people who were putting pressure on him.

"SOMETHING FOR EVERYBODY"

The long-awaited announcement from Secretary Lehman was made on 2 July 1985 in Washington. A Navy spokesman summed up the announcement by saying that there was "something for everybody" in the secretary's plan.[24] Lehman announced that he was increasing the number of ships to be reassigned to the Gulf Coast to 29 and the number of Navy personnel to 15,000 "in a surprise decision that constitutes one of the most major realignments of U.S. Naval power ever."[25] All six finalists were awarded some of the fleet and accompanying personnel, and three cities that had been eliminated earlier from consideration also were included in the final plan.

Lehman announced that the competing cities would serve as homeports for the following ships:

- Mobile—two guided missile destroyers, two guided missile frigates, and one Naval Reserve Force minesweeper.
- Pensacola—one large carrier and one mine warfare ship.
- Pascagoula—two guided missile cruisers and two destroyers.
- Corpus Christi—one battleship (*Wisconsin*), one training carrier, one guided missile cruiser, one destroyer, and one minesweeper.
- Houston/Galveston—two frigates and three minesweepers.
- Lake Charles—two mine warfare ships and one oiler.
- New Orleans—two fast sealift ships.
- Key West—one landing craft repair ship, one salvage ship, and one ocean surveillance ship.
- Gulfport—one mine warfare ship.[26]

New Orleans, Key West, and Gulfport were the three cities that had been eliminated in an earlier round of competition.

Corpus Christi was the biggest winner, because the battleship *Wisconsin* was assigned there. Lehman told the *Houston Post* that the key to deciding to assign the *Wisconsin* to Corpus Christi was its citizens' willingness to pass a referendum to raise $25 million to help defray the cost of building the homeport. He declared that the referendum "tipped the balance" in favor of Corpus Christi. However, he was so impressed with the enthusiasm of other Gulf Coast cities to have the Navy in their communities, "he decided to give something to everyone."[27]

While Lehman continued to say that politics played no part in the homeporting decision, local newspaper articles in the various communities quoted Lehman as crediting Republican members of Congress with bringing the facilities to their cities. For example, in Texas papers, Lehman gave credit to Senator Phil Gramm for bringing Navy homeports to Corpus Christi and to Houston/Galveston:

> Lehman said politics played no part in his decision, but he was willing to declare Gramm, Texas' junior senator, the state's hero of the hour.
>
> "If you rolled up all of the pressure I got from the rest of the Gulf, it didn't nearly amount to what that guy laid on me," Lehman said of the Republican.
>
> Gramm, who held a press conference replete with posters of battleships and aircraft carriers and a picture of a battleship's guns going off to announce the decision, said the most difficult part of his lobbying effort was getting the ships for Houston/Galveston.
>
> The senator said he had to push "hard, hard" to convince the Navy to station auxiliary vessels from the *Wisconsin*'s action group at Fort Point. Pressed to explain what he meant, Gramm said: "I'm not going to give you any of the juicy details. That would be tooting my own horn."[28]

Meanwhile, in the Mobile newspaper, Senator Denton said that Secretary Lehman "'insisted' that he let it be known he [the senator] is responsible for the bonanza to the Gulf Coast."[29] Denton claimed credit for convincing Lehman to create the 15th Carrier Battle Group that was to be spread among the Gulf Coast cities. Other elected officials treated the announcement as a major victory for Mobile. Representative Callahan stated that "this announcement is a supreme compliment to the men and women who so persistently worked on Mobile's proposal. This is great news to our area."[30]

The mood in Pascagoula was reported as jubilant after Representative Trent Lott and Senator John Stennis announced that the Navy had chosen that city to serve as a homeport for two cruisers and two destroyers. Republican Lott explained what happened this way:

> "Lehman knew no matter what he did he stood the chance of making five state congressional delegations mad and I was going to be particularly mad." . . . He found a way to make us all happy."
>
> Lott attributed the increased Gulf Coast ships to three factors: politics, the overwhelming enthusiasm of Gulf Coast cities for Navy homeports and the increasing military strength of Central American countries.
>
> "They were under real political pressure," Lott said of Navy officials making the homeport decision. Because an expansion of the Navy fleet has long been planned, he said, Navy officials showed good military and political sense in doling out portions of the fleet among coast cities.[31]

While Pensacola officials expressed disappointment that they were losing the aircraft carrier *Lexington* to Corpus Christi and that they had expected more ships than they received, the city manager said Lehman's announcement signified "a great day for the entire Gulf Coast."[32]

There were early critics of the plan who saw in Lehman's announcement a blatant political effort to reward congressional friends of the administration and of the Navy. Retired Admiral Eugene Carroll of the Center of Defense Information in Washington stated: "It looks to me almost as if they're planning the election campaign of 1986 with this announcement, enabling all the friends of the administration to go to the public and say, 'Look what wonders I have wrought.'"[33] Another retired admiral, John LaRocque, claimed that Lehman's homeporting plan was simply an effort to "placate the politicians in some of the states."[34]

THE ROAD TO IMPLEMENTATION

In late July 1985, only three weeks after Secretary Lehman announced the selection of the Gulf Coast homeports, the Navy asked the communities for written commitments for part of the construction cost of the homeports. Since the local proposals were designed to handle the battleship group originally identified in the RFP, changes were necessary now to make the proposals conform to the ships that were scheduled for each community. In some cases, the Navy asked for a greater amount of financial support than a community had agreed to in its proposal. For example, the Navy asked Pascagoula for an additional $25 million for waterfront construction such as bulkheads and piers. However, the Navy needed only $7 million for land instead of $13 million and did not require dredging the harbor.[35]

In Mobile, the Navy asked Governor Wallace for written confirmation of Alabama's commitments to build access roads to the site, to provide utilities to the site at no cost, to guarantee availability of adequate private sector housing, to establish and operate a Navy activity center off base, and to assure the Navy of the availability of adequate educational and social services for Navy personnel. In addition, the Navy wanted a commitment for $37 million to purchase the land and construct the necessary waterfront improvements. The mayor of Mobile announced that the task force would do "everything possible to accommodate the Navy" even though some of the task force members did not believe the community was getting its money's worth since the original commitment was based on more ships, more personnel, and more Navy investment. Rather than 3,500 jobs and a $60 million payroll, the Mobile homeport was slated to receive 1,300 jobs and an annual payroll not to exceed $30 million.[36]

The next several years proved to be difficult ones for the homeporting program on the Gulf Coast. The Houston/Galveston and Lake Charles ports were closed in 1988 as a result of the recommendations of the Base Realignment and Closure Commission.[37] By early 1991, the Navy eliminated Pensacola from the homeporting program, leaving only Corpus Christi, Mobile, and Pascagoula. The Navy decided to deactivate the battleship *Wisconsin* that had been assigned to Corpus Christi so it no longer homeported a battleship battlegroup. In addition, the Department of Defense instituted a moratorium on construction of any new facilities from January 1990 to April 1991 which halted work on all of the new homeports.[38]

In Mobile, there was great uncertainty of the homeport's future in early 1990 with reports in the local paper of a shrinking defense budget and fading congressional support for a 600-ship Navy. The Mobile facility was "better than half built" when measured by a financial yardstick, even though most of the new buildings on the new base had not yet been constructed. The state and local commitments to the project had already been made or were well under way by this time.

The *Mobile Press Register* reported:

> The city of Mobile paid its stake early on: $5.4 million to buy the 212 acre site. The Mobile County Commission added $2 million to buy the land and is investing $712,454 to upgrade the roads leading onto the site. . . . About half of the $30 million committed by the state to deepen the channel has been spent. . . . The Mobile Board of Water and Sewer Commissioners paid $754,872 to install water and sewer mains, one-third of which was reimbursed by the Navy.[39]

In early May 1990, Defense Secretary Dick Cheney caused even greater unrest in Mobile, Corpus Christi, and Pascagoula by ordering the immediate suspension of construction projects under way at the homeports. Furthermore, he ordered the Navy to consider canceling the homeports in the three Gulf Coast cities. Senator Richard Shelby of Alabama expressed the concern of Gulf Coast legislators:

> "It seems we are visited by an almost daily list of recommendations and speculations concerning the future of our force structure from the Department of Defense.
>
> Many of the lists contain the names of installations located in the districts and states of those members of Congress who have been strong supporters of national defense. Now is the time for the president and the secretary of defense to win friends and influence people—not give them a daily dose of 'guess what's closing next.'"[40]

Problems for the homeporting program, then, were being created by the secretary of defense, the Base Realignment and Closure Commission, and members of Congress who believed from its inception that the homeporting idea was a bad one. To complicate further the future of the Gulf Coast homeports, an old foe—the General Accounting Office—provided more strong ammunition for homeport opponents.

HOMEPORTING CHALLENGED BY GAO

The GAO had taken a strong stance against the Navy secretary's homeporting plan in its report to the Congress in 1985. By 1990, members of Congress requested GAO to investigate the homeporting program once again and report its findings to the Congress. The request to examine the homeporting program was based in large part on the changes in the world during the five-year period since Lehman announced the new homeports on the Gulf Coast in 1985. Furthermore, Congress's commitment to the 600-ship Navy apparently was dropped when President Reagan and Secretary Lehman left office.

Martin Ferber of the GAO presented a preliminary report of the GAO's study in testimony to Congress in April 1990:

> One objective of the strategic homeporting program was to accommodate about 600 ships, including 15 carrier battlegroups and 4 battleship battlegroups. Today, the Navy has 546 ships, including 14 carrier battlegroups and it plans to retain two of its four battleships. Further expansion of the fleet is not anticipated. In fact, some downsizing is possible.[41]

Ferber told Congress that the 1982 rationale by the Navy to establish strategic homeports was no longer valid. He said the GAO questioned that analysis in 1985 but now felt even more strongly that it was no longer a suitable program for the Navy to pursue. He cited the "changing worldwide threat, declines in the size of the Navy, and budgetary pressures" as reasons to reexamine the homeporting plan.[42]

In June 1991, the GAO transmitted its final report, entitled *Navy Homeports—Expanded Structure Unnecessary and Costly*, to the House Committee on Armed Services. By the time the report was issued, Congress had decided to reduce the size of the Navy even further than earlier projections. The GAO pointed out that the fleet was to be reduced to 464 ships by fiscal year 1993 and to 451 ships by fiscal year 1995. It concluded:

> Therefore, expansion of the fleet and overcrowding no longer serve as valid support. In fact, even if the new homeports are not opened, the existing ports can accommodate the projected number of ships to be berthed there as well as the ships scheduled for the new homeports. . . .
>
> The expanded homeporting structure is not necessary to accommodate the Navy's fleet, most of the original objectives of the strategic homeporting program will not be met, and fiscal realities require reductions in the defense budget. Accordingly, GAO recommends that the new homeports be terminated, and that the Chairman, Defense Base Closure and Realignment Commission, include these homeports in his base closure recommendations to the President.[43]

The Navy responded that it believed that the newer homeports provide "modern piers, maintenance and operational facilities. Quality of life factors, such as family housing, and morale, welfare and recreation facilities provided either by the Navy or existing in the community, are also important factors favoring retention."[44] The Navy recommended to the Base Closure and Realignment Commission that two older homeports be closed instead of the new homeports.

However, by 1993, the Navy and Defense Department agreed that Naval Station Mobile (the official title given to the Mobile homeport) should be closed and recommended its closure to the Base Closure and Realignment Commission. In its *1993 Report to the President*, the commission, in a one-page statement on the Mobile facility, concurred with the recommendation of the secretary of defense that the "capacity to homeport ships at Mobile is excess to that required to support DoD force structure." The commission also concluded that closing the Mobile homeport would have little negative impact on the Mobile economy and would produce savings to the nation of $66.83 million from 1994 to 1999.[45]

Of the six primary cities selected as sites for homeports by Secretary Lehman in 1985, only Corpus Christi and Pascagoula remained by early 1994. David Toenes, the Mobile Chamber of Commerce official who worked with the homeport in Mobile since its inception, predicted that the future for the remaining two homeports was not bright. Senator Heflin disclosed that the Pascagoula homeport would likely be targeted for closing in 1995.[46] If the remaining two facilities are closed as well, then millions of federal and local dollars will have been spent with very little to show for it.

CONCLUSION

Mobile and other Gulf Coast homeport cities were left with unused port facilities with millions of local and federal dollars invested in them after the Navy moved out.[47] Mobile established a commission to determine what the best use of the homeport facility would be. In early 1994, no decision had been made, but the commission was examining several alternatives, including occupancy of the space by the U.S. Coast Guard. The utility of the site for other users was threatened by actions planned by the Navy in March 1994. Alabama's two senators met with Navy Secretary John Dalton and appealed to him to leave the crane on the pier and other equipment from various buildings on the facility.[48]

The Navy's failure to implement fully the homeporting plans of former Navy Secretary Lehman raises a number of interesting points for competitive cities to consider before locating new federal facilities in their communities.

1. Politics apparently plays a large role in the siting of new federal facilities from the beginning of the process to the end of it, if the Gulf Coast homeporting program is typical. The decision to build a new homeport on the Gulf Coast was made by the Reagan administration based on the recommendation of the secretary of the Navy. The choice was either to make improvements to existing homeports in California and Virginia or to build new facilities. Federal, state, and local officials in California and Virginia were anxious to see the existing homeports at San Diego and Norfolk expanded while the officials from the five Gulf Coast states wanted a new homeport built on the Gulf of Mexico coast.

In the case of Mobile, information about the Navy's plans to build the facility was transmitted by Senator Heflin through a news release one year before the request for proposals was issued by the Navy. Once the competing cities' proposals were submitted to the Navy, congressional delegations from all the Gulf Coast states lobbied the secretary and other decision makers in the Department of Defense to locate the homeport in their port communities. Political pressure on the secretary and others appears to have been the reason the Gulf fleet was increased significantly and nine cities were given part of the fleet instead of one city receiving all of it. At the time of the announcements of the homeports, Republican members of Congress—notably, Gramm of Texas, Lott of Mississippi, and Denton of Alabama—were publicly given credit by Lehman for locating parts of the homeport in their states. The personal nature of the political commitments from the Navy secretary to congressional representatives is apparent from Lehman's attempt to give Gramm, Lott, and Denton credit for the location of homeports in their states. Political pressure resulted in "something for everybody," as the Navy spokesman said at the time of the announcement in 1985.

While the political solution developed by the Navy apparently produced nine winners instead of one, the decision to split the ships for the homeport among so many cities may have caused the eventual demise of all of them. If all the resources Congress appropriated to the Navy for the Gulf Coast homeports were concentrated in one facility, it is quite possible that the one homeport would have survived the closings mandated by the Base Closure and Realignment Commission.

2. In addition to the instability caused by political pressures on an administrative agency (such as the Navy in this case), world events can quickly produce changing needs on the part of the federal government. The policy choice by the Reagan administration to increase the Navy's fleet to 600 ships was based on the perceived threat from the Soviet Navy in the early 1980s. The Soviet Navy was larger than the U.S. Navy, and the Reagan administration believed that the United States would not fare well in a naval war with the Soviets. The breakup of the Soviet Union and the dismantling of Communist rule in Eastern Europe in the late 1980s lessened the apparent threat and threw into question the legitimacy of the 600-ship Navy. If communities are asked to contribute millions of dollars for the construction of a federal facility, they need to be aware that national priorities can change based on factors beyond the control of the communities.

3. The relationship between the federal government and the local governments differed in the homeporting case from most federal projects. In this case, the Navy acted much like a private company would in demanding concessions from the localities in order to be considered for the homeport. It was interesting that the Navy's selection process was a public one from the time the request for proposals was issued through the announcement by Secretary Lehman. The case study illustrates that each city engaged important segments of its community in the effort to attract the Navy. For example, in Mobile, a blue-ribbon committee of leading public officials and private-business executives was formed to direct the effort for that city. The local media was kept informed of the committee's progress and journalists were included on tours with Navy officials when they visited Mobile. The high-profile search for a new homeport had the effect of raising the political stakes, especially for the congressional representatives in the five Gulf Coast states. Landing the homeport would be perceived as a major political victory for the senators and representatives and forced them to become even more involved in lobbying the Navy than they otherwise might have been.

   Finally, one wonders what the lost opportunity costs were for the homeport communities. Not only did they and their state governments invest millions of dollars in the Navy facilities, they also invested years of effort by leading public and private officials, as well as their professional economic developers. Possibly, in the long run, the homeport facilities will prove to be worthwhile investments for these communities if other uses are found that produce jobs and economic growth.

NOTES

1. U.S. General Accounting Office, *Navy Ships: Information on Benefits and Costs of Establishing New Homeports* (Washington, D.C.: U.S. General Accounting Office, 1986), 8.

2. Ibid.

3. Frederick H. Hartmann, *Naval Renaissance—The U.S. Navy in the 1980s* (Annapolis, Md.: Naval Institute Press, 1990), 147.

4. U.S. General Accounting Office, *Navy Ships*, 12.

5. Ibid., 8.

6. Tony Germanotta, "Lehman's Homeport Plan Is Labeled Pork-Barreling," *Norfolk (Virginia) Virginian-Pilot*, 22 June 1990, Newsbank 63:C9.

7. Ibid.

8. U.S. General Accounting Office, *Navy Ships*, 11.
9. Ibid., 3.
10. Ibid., 2.
11. U.S. General Accounting Office, *Navy Homeports Expanded Structure Unnecessary and Costly* (Washington, D.C.: U.S. General Accounting Office, 1991), 8.
12. Telephone interview with David Toenes, former homeport coordinator for Mobile, Alabama, on 4 January 1994.
13. David Helms, "Navy Group Tours Pinto Island Site," *Mobile (Alabama) Press Register*, 12 April 1985, Newsbank 30:E11.
14. Hartmann, 146.
15. Leigh Hogan, "Wallace Has $40 Million Ready if Navy Picks Mobile," *Montgomery (Alabama) Journal and Advertiser*, 22 April 1985, Newsbank 30:E12.
16. Ibid.
17. Shawn McIntosh, "Pascagoula Lobbying Hard for Homeport," *Jackson (Mississippi) Clarion-Ledger*, 1 April 1985, Newsbank 30:F2.
18. Ibid.
19. Kathy Kiely, "Tax Vote Wins Corpus Home Port," *Houston (Texas) Post*, 3 July 1985, Newsbank 72:F1.
20. McIntosh, "Pascagoula Lobbying Hard for Homeport," Newsbank 30:F2.
21. Ibid.
22. Ibid.
23. Kathy Kiely, "Home Port Choice Apolitical, Lehman Says," *Houston Post*, 27 June 1985, Newsbank 72:F12.
24. Sandra Baxley Taylor, "Ships Closely Guarded Secret of Sen. Denton, Lehman," *Mobile Press Register*, 3 July 1985, Newsbank 72:E4.
25. Kiely, "Tax Vote Wins Corpus Home Port," Newsbank 72:F1.
26. Taylor, "Ships Closely Guarded Secret of Sen. Denton, Lehman," Newsbank 72:E4.
27. Kiely, Tax Vote Wins Corpus Home Port," Newsbank 72:F1.
28. Ibid.
29. Taylor, "Ships Closely Guarded Secret of Sen. Denton, Lehman," Newsbank 72:E4.
30. Ibid.
31. Shawn McIntosh, "Battleship Goes to Texas; 2 State Ports Assigned Ships," *Jackson Clarion Ledger*, 3 July 1985, Newsbank 72:E6.
32. Taylor, "Ships Closely Guarded Secret of Sen. Denton, Lehman," Newsbank 72:E4.
33. Richard Whittle, "Corpus Chosen as Home Port," *Dallas (Texas) Morning News*, 3 July 1985, Newsbank 72:F6.
34. Germanotta, "Lehman's Plan Is Labeled Pork-Barreling," Newsbank 63:C9.

35. Shawn McIntosh, "Navy Asks Pascagoula for Construction Funds," *Jackson Clarion Ledger*, 20 July 1985, Newsbank 72:F14.

36. David Helms, "'Great Ships on Horizon,'" *Mobile Press Register*, 24 July 1985, Newsbank 72:F14.

37. U.S. Congress, House Committee on Armed Services, *Report of the Defense Secretary's Committee on Base Realignment and Closure on Armed Services*, 101st Cong., 1st Sess., 22 February and 1 March, 1988, 434–35.

38. U.S. General Accounting Office, *Navy Homeports Expanded Structure Unnecessary and Costly* (Washington, D.C.: U.S. General Accounting Office, 1991), 35.

39. Royce Harrison, "Work at Naval Station Mobile Continues Despite Uncertain Future," *Mobile Press Register*, 16 April 1990, Newsbank 38:G6.

40. Thomas Hargrove, "Cheney Puts Halt on Base in Mobile," *Birmingham (Alabama) News*, 2 May 1990, Newsbank 49:G8.

41. U.S. General Accounting Office, *Navy Ships: Status of Strategic Homeporting Program* (Washington, D.C.: U.S. General Accounting Office, 1990), 4–5.

42. Ibid.

43. General Accounting Office, *Navy Homeports*, 3–5.

44. Ibid., 5.

45. U.S. Defense Base Closure and Realignment Commission, *1993 Report to the President* (Washington, D.C.: U.S. Defense Base Closure and Realignment Commission, 1993), I-32.

46. Frank Sikora, "Mobile Base Closing Said Fastest in History," *Birmingham News/Post Herald*, 26 March 1994, 5A and 8A.

47. David Pace, "Senators Seek Moratorium," *Montgomery Advertiser*, 5 March 1994, 3F.

48. Ibid.

8 Final Thoughts

This book has presented evidence that the competition among state and local governments for economic development is becoming more and more intense. The new civil war that states are waging for major economic development prizes, such as the Mercedes-Benz plant in Alabama, the BMW plant in South Carolina, and the United Airlines maintenance facility in Indianapolis, shows no signs of abating. The changing world economy has placed a premium on high-paying manufacturing, commercial, and government jobs, so state and local governments are willing to go to great lengths to be competitive with other jurisdictions. Furthermore, the political benefits to the elected officials who land major projects appear to be substantial and provide an incentive to governors and mayors to use state or local government resources to be competitive for development.

Stockman, Friedman, and others have questioned whether government has any role in economic development other than its traditional ones, such as providing infrastructure and ensuring honesty in the market. Many argue that not only is it inappropriate for government to be so heavily involved in the market but that it has no significant effect on making American industries more productive or competitive. However, these critics are missing the point of why state and local governments are involved in economic development. It is not to further national goals of making American industry more competitive in world markets but to create jobs, investment, and taxes in their jurisdictions. The goals are strictly local ones. If there is a benefit to the nation in promoting American business in world markets, it is of secondary interest to state and local economic developers.

The entrepreneurial efforts of state and local governments have changed the relationship between the public and private sectors in the United States. The lines between the two have become even more blurred as the competition among governments has increased. State and local governments are acting much like the private sector in the new roles they have assumed. For example, the Alabama cities of Auburn and Bessemer are using revolving loan funds and other financing techniques to invest in facilities for companies in order to make it attractive to locate in their communities. The local governments have a strong financial interest in the success of the companies they attract and generally are willing to help the companies in other ways to ensure that they stay in the communities. Another example is the incentives law passed by the state of Alabama, described in the Mercedes-Benz case study that allows the employees' income taxes owed to the state to be used by the company to pay the debt service on manufacturing buildings. In effect, proponents argue, the state is building facilities for companies by foregoing tax dollars that it would not have received anyway had the companies not located in Alabama.

The point is that state and local governments have gone beyond their traditional roles of regulators and tax collectors or even that of providers of infrastructure for industry. They are now investors and partners in businesses that create jobs and generate taxes for them. The question of whether this is a necessary and appropriate role for state and local governments was addressed in chapter 1. The generally accepted view of state and local officials is that economic development is a legitimate role for them. Governors and mayors spend a substantial amount of their time and effort on economic development, as is obvious from both the case studies presented in this book and a casual reading of any local newspaper.

An important question is whether the competition among governments for economic development has any limits. Is there any mechanism available to stop states and localities from creating financial liabilities they cannot afford? It seems unlikely that Congress will make any move to regulate the incentives that state and local governments are willing to give companies. As long as states are not giving away taxes from the federal treasury, Congress is likely to believe that state legislatures are free to use their own resources in any way they choose. The other possibility is an agreement among the states to limit the incentives offered to companies. The National Governors' Association has proposed a compact to accomplish that, but it apparently has had little impact on the actions of the states. It appears nearly impossible to obtain a consensus of fifty governors, fifty state legislatures, and the numerous other state and local agencies that are involved in economic development to limit the incentives war. Since states and localities are in competition, it is almost certain that governments will act in their own self-interest when the opportunity is present to attract major economic development projects.

If a majority of citizens believe that the competition has gone too far and that their tax dollars are being used to subsidize the private sector without sufficient return to them, then governors, mayors, and legislatures will limit the incentives war. During the nineteenth century, there was a strong reaction to the subsidies offered by governments to railroads and other companies. This reaction led to limits on the role of government in using its resources for economic development that lasted until the 1930s, when Mississippi initiated the use of industrial development bonds. While there has been some negative public reaction to the incentive packages offered by various states in the more heavily publicized competitions for major projects in recent years, there does not appear yet to be enough citizen opposition to slow the incentives wars.

Selected Bibliography

Babcock, Richard F. "The City as Entrepreneur: Fiscal Wisdom or Regulatory Folly?" in Terry Jill Lassar, ed., *City Deal Making*. Washington, D.C.: Urban Land Institute, 1990, 9–43.

Bellone, Carl J., and George Frederick Goerl. "In Defense of Civic-Regarding Entrepreneurship, or Helping Wolves to Promote Good Citizenship." *Public Administration Review* 53, no. 4 (July/August 1993): 396–98.

Bowman, Ann O'M. "Competition for Economic Development among Southeastern Cities." *Urban Affairs Quarterly* 23, no. 4 (June 1988): 511–27.

Burkhalter, Bettye, Douglas J. Watson, and Jamie Sinclair. "The Role of Speculative Buildings in Small Community Industrial Development." Auburn, Ala.: Economic Development Institute, 1991.

Byram, Jim. "Preservation of Capital as a Tool in Economic Development." Thesis, Economic Development Institute, University of Oklahoma, 1993.

Cobb, James C. *The Selling of the South*. Urbana, Ill.: University of Illinois Press, 1993.

Conway, H. McKinley. *Marketing Industrial Buildings and Sites*. Atlanta: Conway Publications, 1980.

Duckworth, Robert P., John M. Simmons, and Robert H. McNulty. *The Entrepreneurial American City*. Washington, D.C.: Partners for Livable Places and the U.S. Department of Housing and Urban Development, 1986.

Dunlap, T. Phillip, Bettye B. Burkhalter, Douglas J. Watson, and Jacki A. Fitzpatrick. "Reshaping the Local Economy through a Revolving

Loan Fund in an Entrepreneurial City." *Economic Development Quarterly*, forthcoming.

Farr, Cheryl. "Encouraging Local Economic Development: The State of the Practice." In International City Management Association, *The Municipal Year Book 1990.* Washington, D.C.: International City Management Association, 1990: 15–29.

Foster, Wayne. *Speculative Buildings: A Tool for Industrial Development.* Jackson, Miss.: Mississippi Research and Development Center, 1977.

Galbraith, J. Kenneth. *Age of Uncertainty.* Boston: Houghton Mifflin, 1977.

Goldstein, Harvey A., and Michael I. Luger. "University-based Research Parks as a Rural Development Strategy." *Policy Studies Journal* 20, no. 2 (1992): 249–63.

Green, C. Warren. "Shell Building Experiences of Eleven Rural Virginia Communities: 1979–1990." *Economic Development Review* 9, no. 4 (Fall 1991): 78–82.

Greider, William. *The Education of David Stockman and Other Americans.* New York: E. P. Dutton, 1981.

Harrigan, John J. *Political Change in the Metropolis,* 3d ed. Boston: Little, Brown, 1985.

Hartmann, Frederick H. *Naval Renaissance—The U.S. Navy in the 1980s.* Annapolis, Md.: Naval Institute Press, 1990.

Heilman, John G., and Gerald W. Johnson. *The Politics and Economics of Privatization.* Tuscaloosa, Ala.: University of Alabama Press, 1992.

International City Management Association. *Recycling CDBG and UDAG Funds.* Washington, D.C.: Management Information Publications, 1991.

Lehman, John F., Jr. *Command of the Seas.* New York: Charles Scribner's Sons, 1988.

Luger, Michael I., and Harvey A. Goldstein. *Technology in the Garden.* Chapel Hill, N.C.: University of North Carolina Press, 1991.

Lyons, Thomas S., and Roger E. Hamlin. *Creating an Economic Development Plan.* New York: Praeger Publishers, 1991.

Moore, Thomas J., and Gregory D. Squires. "Industrial Revenue Bonds: The Social Costs and Private Benefits of a Public Subsidy." *Public Administration Quarterly* 12, no. 2 (Summer 1988): 151–68.

Palmintera, Diane. *Local- and Regional-based Initiatives to Increase Productivity, Technology, and Innovation.* Washington, D.C.: Innovation Associates, 1991.

Peterson, John, Susan Robinson, Percy Aquila, Joni Leithe, and William Graham. *Credit Pooling to Finance Infrastructure: An Examination of State Bond Banks, Revolving Loan Funds, and Substate Credit Pools.* Washington, D.C.: Government Finance Research Center, 1988.

Pierce, Lee Ann. "Tax Exempt Bonds." *South Dakota Law Review* 32, no. 3 (1987): 525–33.

Rollinson, Mark. *Small Issue Industrial Development Bonds.* Chicago: Capital Publishing, 1976.

Rymarowicz, Lillian, and Dennis Zimmerman. "Federal Budget and Tax Policy and the State-Local Sector: Retrenchment in the 1980s." *CRS Report for Congress.* Washington, D.C.: Library of Congress, 9 September 1988.

Rymph, David, and Jack Underhill. *Analysis of Income Earned from UDAG Projects.* Washington, D.C.: U.S. Department of Housing and Urban Development, 1990.

Shannon, John. "The Return to Fend-for-Yourself Federalism: The Reagan Mark." *Intergovernmental Perspective* 13 (Summer/Fall 1987): 34–37.

Sharp, Elaine B. *Urban Politics and Administration.* New York: Longman, 1990.

Smith, Robert G. *Political Authorities in Urban Areas: A Case Study of Special District Government.* Washington, D.C.: National Association of Counties, 1969.

Stoker, Robert P. "Baltimore: The Self-Evaluating City?" in Clarence N. Stone and Heywood T. Sanders, eds., *The Politics of Urban Development.* Lawrence, Kans.: University of Kansas Press, 1987, 244–66.

Syed, Anwar. *The Political Theory of American Local Government.* New York: Random House, 1969.

Terry, Larry D. "Why We Should Abandon the Misconceived Quest to Reconcile Public Entrepreneurship with Democracy." *Public Administration Review* 53, no. 4 (July/August 1993): 393–95.

U.S. Advisory Commission on Intergovernmental Relations. *Regional Decision Making: New Strategies for Sub-state Districts.* Washington, D.C.: U.S. Government Printing Office, 1973.

U.S. Congress. House Committee on Armed Services. *Report of the Defense Secretary's Commission on Base Realignment and Closure.* 101st Cong., 1st Sess., 22 February and 1 March 1989.

U.S. Congress. Senate Committee on Small Business. *Small Issue Industrial Development Bonds: Hearings before the Subcommittee on Small Business: Family Farm.* 99th Cong., 1st Sess., 11 June 1985.

U.S. Defense Base Closure and Realignment Commission. *1993 Report to the President.* Washington, D.C.: Defense Base Closure and Realignment Commission, 1993.

U.S. Department of Defense. Office of Economic Adjustment. *Civilian Reuse of Former Military Bases.* Washington, D.C.: U.S. Department of Defense, 1993.

U.S. Department of Housing and Urban Development. Office of Community Planning and Development. *Report to Congress on Community Development Programs—1989.* Washington, D.C.: U.S. Department of Housing and Urban Development, 1989.

U.S. General Accounting Office. *Navy Homeports Expanded Structure Unnecessary and Costly.* Washington, D.C.: U.S. General Accounting Office, 1991.

U.S. General Accounting Office. *Navy Ships: Information on Benefits and Costs of Establishing New Homeports.* Washington, D.C.: U.S. General Accounting Office, 1986.

Watson, Douglas J. "Importance of Local Initiative in Targeting of Federal Aid: The Case of UDAGs." *Public Budgeting and Financial Management*, forthcoming.

Watson, Douglas J., John G. Heilman, and Robert S. Montjoy. *The Politics of Redistributing Urban Aid.* Westport, Conn.: Praeger Publishers, 1994.

Watson, Douglas J., and Thomas Vocino. "The Changing Nature of Intergovernmental Fiscal Relationships: The Impact of the 1986 Tax Reform Act on State and Local Governments." *Public Administration Review* 50, no. 4 (1990): 427–34.

Wilson, Roger. *State Business Incentives and Economic Growth: Are They Effective? A Review of the Literature.* Lexington, Ky.: Council of State Governments, 1989.

Wolf, Charles, Jr. *Markets or Governments.* Cambridge: MIT Press, 1988.

Zimmerman, Dennis. "Tax Reform: Its Potential Effect on the State and Local Sector." *CRS Report for Congress.* Washington, D.C.: Library of Congress, 20 March 1987.

Index

About the Author

DOUGLAS J. WATSON has been a city manager for the past twenty years and has been involved with local economic development during that time. He has written articles and books on the subject of urban aid, management, and economic development, including *The Politics of Redistributing Urban Aid* (Praeger, 1994).

HARDCOVER BAR CODE